D0852964

Mount Sneffels Range

Photo by Jack Olson

COLORADO
HIGH COUNTRY COOKING

LEISURE
TIME
PUBLISHING
INC.
DALLAS,TX

Copyright © 1990 by Leisure Time Publishing, Incorporated, Dallas, Texas

All rights reserved. No part of this book may be reproduced in any form or by any means without permission in writing from the authors or publishers.

Published by the Colorado Department of Agriculture, Denver, Colorado, in association with Leisure Time Publishing, a division of Heritage Worldwide, Incorporated, Dallas, Texas.

Publisher: Rodney L. Dockery
General Manager & Editorial Director: Caleb Pirtle III
Executive Editor: Ken Lively
Managing Editor: Sheri Harris

Regional Publishing Director: P.K. Dailey
Project Editor: Betty Miser
Food Editor: Diane Luther
Editorial Assistants: Patti Griffith
                                                    Susan Lee
Art Director: Lynn Herndon Sullivan
Production Coordinator: Erin Gregg
Production Manager: Vickie Craig

Contributing authors: Mary Lou Chapman, and Herb Jackson.

Photography provided by the Colorado Tourism Board, the Breckenridge Ski Corporation, and © photos by Jeff Andrew, Art Bilsten, Gerald Brimacombe, Anne Krause, Jack Olson, Larry Pierce, Lou Poulter, Ron Ruhoff, Smokey Vandergrift, and Bob Winsett.

Cover Photograph: Mount Sneffels in the San Juan Mountains near Ridgway, Colorado © Jeff Andrew.

First Printing

Manufactured in the United States of America

Printed by:
Heritage Worldwide, Inc.
9029 Directors Row
Dallas, Texas 75247
Telephone: (214) 630-4300

CONTENTS

FOREWORD

Rich. Distinctive. Flavorful. Robust. Words that are as descriptive of Colorado as they are of fine cooking. And that's what Colorado's High Country Cooking is all about.

Colorado has its own distinctive heritage and the following recipes mirror the best cooking that Colorado has to offer. They were developed by Coloradans for Coloradans, using Colorado-made food products.

We certainly appreciate the time and effort each Colorado food producer and manufacturer took in the creation of these favorite recipes. And, in order to create a broader awareness of the many great products made in the state and to benefit you in your efforts to support them, the publisher has provided the brand names of Colorado products for many of the ingredients in the recipes.

So sit back and savor this book. It's a dash of the Old West, a sip of clear water, a breath of fresh air, a taste of Colorado.

Bon voyage. Bon appétit.

APPETIZERS & SNACKS

Storm at Sunset, Rabbit Ears Pass overlooking Yampa Valley

Photo by Smokey Vandergrift

CHANGING COLORADO

The change which took place in Colorado during its formative years was enormous. Poet Vachel Lindsay, commented:

The flower-fed buffaloes of the spring
In the days of long ago,
Ranged where the locomotives sing
And the prairie flowers lie low;
The tossing, blooming, perfumed grass
Is swept away by wheat,
Wheels and wheels and wheels spin by
In the spring that still is sweet.
But the flower-fed buffaloes of the spring
Left us long ago.
They gore no more, they bellow no more,
They trundle around the hills no more:
With the Blackfeet lying low,
With the Pawnees lying low.

Creole Dip

1 (8 oz) pkg cream cheese
1 cup sour cream
2½ tsp Lucile's Famous Creole Seasoning
¼ tsp hot pepper sauce
1 lemon, juiced
⅓ cup finely chopped pears or apples
raw vegetables, apples or crackers

- Thoroughly mix first 5 ingredients in a food processor or blender.
- Remove from blender to bowl and, by hand, stir in pears or apples.
- Serve with raw vegetables, apples or crackers.
- Makes 2½ cups.

ELVES IN THE MINES

Tommyknockers—say what? Around any industry superstitions arise. The Colorado mining industry was no different. Thus, the advent of Tommyknockers, said to be elf-like creatures who lived in the mines. Not many actually saw the little folk, but they could be heard. Two types seemed to exist—friendly ones and mischievous ones. The former helped miners, even saving their lives; the latter always screwed things up. Tommyknockers seemed to be around two-feet tall, wore colorful shirts and were believed to be the souls of departed miners. With long beards, large heads and wrinkled faces, their tapping on the mine walls between midnight and 2 a.m. could lead miners to a rich vein of ore. Miners tried to stay on the good side of the Tommyknockers. They even left food for them. It's believed that the Tommyknockers were brought to Colorado by Cornish miners from England.

Hot Broccoli Dip

1 (1 lb) loaf Schmidt's Round French Bread

½ cup finely chopped celery

½ cup finely chopped onion

2 tbsp margarine

1 lb processed cheese spread, cubed

1 (10 oz) pkg frozen chopped broccoli, thawed and drained

¼ tsp crushed Bellwether Farms Rosemary Leaves

raw vegetables

- Cut slice from top of bread loaf; remove center, leaving 1" shell.
- Cut removed bread into bite-size pieces.
- Sauté celery and onion in margarine until tender.
- Add cheese; stir over low heat until cheese is melted.
- Stir in remaining ingredients except vegetables; heat thoroughly, stirring constantly.
- Spoon into hollowed bread loaf.
- Serve with raw vegetables or bread.
- Makes 3 cups.

BRANDS AND BARBED WIRE

Barbed wire and branding were two major accomplishments in the development of Colorado's cattle industry. Ranchers attempted to keep their animals in one section until the fall when they could be branded, culled and then turned loose for the winter to graze on their own. The brands then helped to identify a rancher's herd during the spring roundups. Obviously, this method left plenty of room for rustlers to steal animals from the herd. It was unhealthy to be caught with suspiciously altered brands.

As the face of the range changed, homesteaders began to look for ways of keeping out wandering cattle. They tried smooth fencing, solid fences and hedges, but nothing really worked until Joseph Glidden began manufacturing his double-strand barbed wire fencing in 1874. That type of fence even the orneriest Colorado steer had to respect.

Chili Dip

1 (8 oz) pkg cream cheese, softened
1 (15 oz) jar Championship Recipe Chili
No Beans
grated Cheddar cheese
assorted chips and crackers

- Scoop cream cheese into the center of a medium microwave bowl.
- Pour chili on top of cream cheese.
- Microwave on MEDIUM 3-4 minutes, until cheese begins to melt.
- Stir mixture.
- Sprinkle grated Cheddar cheese on top; microwave an additional 2-4 minutes, until both the Cheddar and the cream cheese have melted.
- Serve as a centerpiece for chips and crackers for dipping.
- Serves 8-10.

SPORTS-HAPPY COLORADO

As one might expect in a state with so much natural beauty, Coloradans are a sports loving people. Whether it is the action of skiing, the serenity of hiking and camping, the solitude of fishing, the challenge of rock climbing, the thrill of white water rafting or the joy of so many other sports, people living in Colorado take their participation seriously. Those strong competitive instincts are translated to their support of their professional, college, high school and independent sports teams. Possibly it is the frontier spirit, that makes today's Coloradans immerse themselves so directly into sports. Whatever it is that drives this spirit, visitors, or those just moving into the state, soon catch it and participate. It is hearty living for a very hearty people.

Low Calorie Curry Dip

1 (15 oz) ctn Chapin's Supreme Curry Sauce
1 cup Mountain High® Plain Yoghurt
raw vegetables, sliced

- Mix curry sauce and yoghurt together.
- Serve with a variety of raw vegetables.
- Makes 1½ cups.

Pepper Jelly Spread

1 (8 oz) pkg cream cheese
1 (10 oz) jar Joy's Chili Jelly, Hot or Mild
assorted crackers

- Put block of cream cheese in deep plate.
- Cover with jelly.
- Serve with crackers.
- Serves 8-10.

WHERE A FEW BUFFALO ROAM

The plains of Colorado have run black with buffalo. But in time, hunters wanted only to slaughter the shaggy animals, decimating the herds. Yet today's Colorado visitor can still experience the majesty of this noble beast. Follow Interstate 70 west of Denver and you will arrive at an area known as Genesee Park. There, on a rolling hillside, graze a small herd of buffalo, maintained by the City of Denver. In the spring their red-coated calves can be seen playing together or nursing their mothers.

Across the modern highway from the herd's primary grazing area is a windmill and a trough used for watering these animals along with elk that are also kept in the park. From behind the fence line, you can usually get quite a good glimpse of the buffalos in their natural habitat.

Chili-Cheese Log

1 (8 oz) pkg cream cheese

1 lb shredded Cheddar cheese

2 tbsp mayonnaise

1 tbsp More Than Mustard Original Recipe Mustard

2 tsp F & J Mesquite Worcestershire Sauce

2 tbsp Dixon & Sons Q-Mix

crackers, melba toast or bread sticks

- Beat cheeses, mayonnaise, mustard and Worcestershire sauce together until smooth.
- Roll into 2 logs the width of a round cracker.
- Sprinkle waxed paper with Q-Mix. Roll each log in the Q-Mix until covered. Wrap in plastic wrap.
- Chill 3-4 days to blend flavors.
- Serve with assorted crackers, toast or bread sticks.
- Serves 12-16.

AN INDUSTRY IN BLOOM

Colorado annually sells 85 million carnations at a value of $12 million outside the state. Annual rose sales outside of Colorado total 61 million at a value exceeding $8 million. Over 17,000 people work in Colorado greenhouses. Total annual sales from Colorado's retail garden centers is $12 million. The figures could go on, but the point is evident—an industry that many of us may not even consider to be a part of agriculture, actually contributes enormously to its revenues and that of the state as a whole. Thank a Colorado rose next time you have the chance.

Dilly Dip

1½ cups Meadow Gold Sour Cream
½ cup mayonnaise
1 tbsp dillweed
1 tbsp parsley flakes
1½ tbsp chopped red onion
1 tsp lemon juice
½ tsp garlic powder
2 tbsp Colorado Gold Mustard
raw vegetables, sliced

- Mix all ingredients, except vegetables, together; refrigerate.
- Serve chilled with vegetables.
- Makes 2½ cups.

Sausage in a Blanket

1 can croissant dough
1 (1 lb) pkg Old West Smoked Polish, Hot Polish, Extra Hot Polish, German, Italian, Chorizo or Cajun Sausage
5 slices cheese (Swiss, Monterey Jack or Cheddar)

- Unroll the croissant dough; place sausage and slice of cheese on dough.
- Roll up.
- Place on cookie sheet and bake according to pkg directions.
- Serves 5.

SEEING THE BEST SIGHTS

Mountain and plains sites well worth seeing when traveling throughout Colorado's high country: Big Thompson Canyon near Loveland/Estes Park; Key Hole in Long's Peak Trail near Estes Park; Mount of the Holy Cross southwest of Vail; Seven Falls near Colorado Springs; Mount Garfield near Grand Junction; the Currecanti Needle in the Black Canyon of the Gunnison River near Montrose; Red Rock Amphitheatre near Morrison; Balanced Rock and Steamboat Rock at the Garden of the Gods; Grand Lake near Granby; the chalk cliffs of Chalk Creek Canyon northwest of Salida; Fisher's Peak near Trinidad; Sheepshead Rock in the Big Thompson Canyon; Vail Pass; Pikes Peak; Royal Gorge; Independence Pass; Florissant Fossil Beds near Colorado Springs; Great Sand Dunes near Alamosa; Dillon Lake; the Snow Angel on Mount Shavano west and north of Salida and many, many more.

Hot & Spicy Bison Meatballs in Cranberry Sauce

1 egg, beaten
1 medium Tateys Onion, finely diced
2 lbs Lay Valley Bison Ranch Ground Buffalo Meat
vegetable oil
1 (16 oz) can jellied cranberry sauce
3 tbsp prepared horseradish
2 tbsp Lucky Clover Honey
1 tbsp Worcestershire sauce
1 tbsp lemon juice
1 clove garlic, minced
½ tsp Ground Red Pepper

- Add egg and onion to ground buffalo meat; mix well. Form into bite-size balls.
- Brown in oil.
- In medium saucepan, combine remaining ingredients.
- Bring to a boil; reduce heat and simmer, covered, 5 minutes.
- Add meatballs; heat.
- Serve hot.
- Serves 10-15.

Zippy Pinto Bean Dip

1 cup mashed Red Bird Brand
Pinto Beans
1 cup ketchup
½ cup finely cut sweet pickles
1 tsp finely cut onions (optional)
1 tbsp sugar
¼ tsp savory salt
¼ tsp Colorado Spice Co. Garlic Salt
¼ tsp Colorado Spice Co. Celery Salt
Bravo Nacho Chips

- Combine all ingredients, except chips.
- Serve with chips.
- Makes 2 cups.

Smoked Trout Ball

1 (3 oz) can Colorado Rainbow Smoked
Trout, flaked
1 (8 oz) pkg cream cheese, softened
3 tbsp chopped onion
1 clove garlic, minced
1 tbsp lemon juice
1 tbsp F & J Worcestershire Sauce
1 tbsp horseradish (optional)
chopped parsley
assorted crackers

- Combine all ingredients except parsley and crackers.
- Form into ball. Roll in parsley.
- Chill.
- Can be made 2-3 days ahead to let the flavors blend.
- Serve with assorted crackers.
- Serves 8-10.

Sausage Stuffed Mushrooms

1 lb large Rakhra Mushrooms, washed
and trimmed
1 lb Canino's Sausage
grated Parmesan cheese

- Fill mushrooms with sausage; pat until sausage is mounded and secure.
- Sprinkle with Parmesan cheese.
- Bake on ungreased cookie sheet at 350 degrees 30 minutes.
- Serve hot.
- Serves 20.

BACKPACKING TO BACK COUNTRY

Another reason so many people visit Colorado each year is the unexcelled backpacking and camping. An estimated 13 million acres is preserved for your camping enjoyment. And camping, or back country hiking in Colorado is the real thing. All outdoors, wrapped in the silence of the primeval forest. Indian Country that gets you back to nature. Rushing streams filled with Rocky Moutain trout, or grand vistas you cannot find any other way than to pack up your gear and go into the back country. You have not really camped out until you've pitched your tent in the mountain expanse of Colorado.

Holiday Buttercorn

16 cups Roberts Popped Popcorn
1 cup pecan halves
1 cup blanched whole almonds
1 cup walnut halves
2 cups firmly packed GW Dark Brown Sugar
1 cup Rocky Mountain Butter
½ cup dark corn syrup
½ tsp salt
½ tsp baking soda

- Preheat oven to 250 degrees.
- Put popcorn and nuts in a large roasting pan. Keep warm in a 250 degree oven.
- Put brown sugar, butter, syrup and salt in a large saucepan. Bring to boil, stirring constantly. Stop stirring and cook to 250 degrees on candy thermometer, 5 minutes.
- Stir baking soda into caramel. Drizzle over popcorn; toss to coat.
- Bake in 250 degree oven 5-10 minutes. For crispier corn, bake 15-20 minutes.
- Makes 20 cups.

Hi-Country Trail Mix

½ cup Colorado Poppin Gold Popcorn, popped

1 cup Leroux Creek Raisins

1 cup Naturally Nuts Peanuts

1 cup sunflower seeds

1 cup pretzel sticks

- Mix all ingredients with fresh popped popcorn.
- Put in sealed lock bags to make snack packs.
- Makes 2 qts.

Colorado Honey Popcorn

½ cup Ambrosia Honey

½ cup melted Royal Crest Butter

¼ tsp nutmeg

½ cup Colorado Poppin Gold Popcorn, popped

¼ cup raisins or peanuts (optional)

- Heat honey in saucepan, being careful not to boil.
- Mix with melted butter and nutmeg.
- In separate bowl, mix popped popcorn with raisins or peanuts.
- Pour honey mixture over popcorn and raisins or peanuts; mix well.
- Heat oven to 300 degrees.
- Spread mixture on cookie sheet; bake 10-15 minutes.
- Makes 2 qts.

Curried Apple Dip

1½ cups Mountain High® Honey Vanilla or Plain Yoghurt

1 cup shredded Colorado Apple

⅓ cup shredded President's Pride Extra Sharp Cheddar Cheese

¼ cup chopped nuts

¼ cup Leroux Creek Raisins

¼ tsp curry powder

apples, assorted raw vegetables or crackers

- In small bowl, combine first 6 ingredients.
- Cover; chill 2 hours to blend flavors.
- Serve with apples, assorted raw vegetables or crackers.
- Makes 3 cups.

BREADS

Colorful Keystone

Photo by Bob Winsett

PRAIRIE GOLD

A major event takes place each summer in Colorado. The event is not held in a sports arena, but, rather, is played out in fields of wavy golden wheat. Wheat harvest is an event of considerable importance to the state's economy. The wheat industry accounts for more than $300 million directly to the Colorado economy. When the jobs created in related areas such as milling, baking, farm equipment, fertilizer, transportation and retail sales are added, the figure multiplies nearly four-fold, for a total impact in Colorado of over a billion dollars. The big figures explain why the state's wheat farmers refer to their product as "Prairie Gold." The major wheat-growing regions are located in the eastern half of the state, plus some acreage in the northwestern quadrant. The average wheat farm is about 1,100 acres. Colorado wheat is predominantly winter wheat, which is adapted to the state's arid climate, and is especially suited for bread and all-purpose flour that requires high protein content.

Layered French Toast

Ingredients	Instructions
2 eggs	• Preheat non-stick griddle or skillet.
⅔ cup Royal Crest 2% Milk	• Combine eggs, milk, vanilla, salt, cinnamon and sweetener.
½ tsp vanilla	
pinch salt	• Pour into flat pan and dip bread slices, turning quickly. Immediately cook until lightly browned on each side. Repeat with remaining bread.
¼ tsp cinnamon	
2 pkgs sweetener	
12 slices Earth Grains Very Thin Wheat Bread	• For each serving, place 1 slice French toast on warmed plate; add ⅓ cup strawberries, 1 slice toast, ⅓ cup bananas, 1 slice toast, then ⅓ cup peaches. Top each serving with 2 tbsp syrup and 2 tbsp whipped topping.
1⅓ cups sliced strawberries	
1⅓ cups sliced bananas	
1⅓ cups Colorado Peaches	
½ cup light syrup	• Serves 4.
½ cup whipped topping	

A BLUE SPRUCE CHRISTMAS

The official state tree of Colorado is the Colorado Blue Spruce, native to only a few states in the Central Rockies. This magnificent tree enjoys widespread popularity throughout the world as a favorite ornamental. At Christmas, the nation can enjoy the Blue Spruce covered with lights on the lawn in front of the White House. First introduced in 1862, the Blue Spruce is characterized by sharp, distinctly blue-colored foliage. Its needles are stiff and sharp. A waxy coating on the needles gives the tree its unusual frosted appearance.

Winterfest Stollen

1 pkg active dry yeast
½ cup Coors Winterfest Beer*
3½ cups all-purpose flour, divided
1 cup butter, softened
½ cup sugar
1 egg
1 tsp salt
½ tsp almond extract
peel of ½ lemon
1 cup raisins
⅓ cup chopped candied fruit
¾ cup marzipan
melted butter
2 oz powdered sugar

*Winterfest may be substituted with another Coors beer.

- Dissolve yeast in beer; add ½ cup flour; let rise.
- Cream butter with sugar; add egg, salt, almond extract and lemon peel.
- Mix raisins and candied fruit with ½ cup flour.
- Add yeast mixture to butter mixture; add remaining 2½ cups flour. Knead until smooth and elastic.
- Sprinkle dried fruit over top and knead in.
- Shape into ball and put into greased bowl.
- Let rise until doubled. Toss on floured board.
- Divide into 2 loaves. Roll into square and lay marzipan on top; cover well with dough. Place on cookie sheet.
- Allow to rise; bake in 350 degree oven 45 minutes.
- While still warm, brush top with melted butter and dust with powdered sugar.
- Serves 16-20.

BRINGING IN THE APPLE TREES

The first recorded Colorado apple yields and shipments are dated 1910. In the tradition of American pioneers, early settlers, who arrived after the departure of the Ute Indians in 1881, brought fruit trees with them in their wagons. Before they could plant their orchards they had to clear the land of the huge rock deposits that covered the area. The large rock "walls" still remain, marking property lines. Early varieties of apples, including Jonathan and Winesap, were carried to the miners by itinerant peddlers. The extension of the railroads into the area provided growers with a method of shipping their products.

Apple Strawberry Kanten

3 bars kanten (agar-agar)
or
8 tbsp flakes
4½ cups Mountain Sun Apple Juice
1½ cups water
2 tsp Colorado Spice Co. Vanilla
2½ cups strawberries
2 tbsp tahini
walnuts to garnish

- In saucepan, combine kanten, apple juice and water. Bring to boil and simmer until dissolved completely. Stir in vanilla.
- While simmering, wash and clean strawberries; then cut each lengthwise into several slices.
- Line bottom of 9" shallow square or rectangular baking pan with ⅔ of the strawberries, setting remainder aside in another pan or bowl.
- Gently pour hot kanten mixture over strawberries to depth of 1½"; pour remaining kanten over other berries. Chill both until set.
- To serve, cut kanten in baking pan into 6 pieces.
- Transfer second kanten to blender, add tahini and puree until smooth.
- Serve as sauce over kanten squares. Top with walnuts.
- Serve remaining puree for breakfast.
- Serves 6-8.

Campfire Coffee Cake

Cake:
½ cup Meadow Gold Butter, softened

1½ cups Holly Granulated Sugar

2 eggs

1 cup Meadow Gold Sour Cream

1 tsp vanilla

2 cups Hungarian® All-Purpose Flour

½ tsp baking soda

1 tsp baking powder

Topping:
½ cup Holly Light Brown Sugar

¼ cup Holly Granulated Sugar

2 tsp cinnamon

2 tbsp Hungarian® All-Purpose Flour

2½ tbsp Meadow Gold Butter

½ cup chopped Naturally Nuts Pecans

- Preheat oven to 350 degrees.
- Grease and flour 9″ x 13″ pan.
- Cream together butter and sugar.
- Add eggs, 1 at a time, beating well after each addition.
- Add sour cream and vanilla, mixing well.
- Sift together flour, baking soda and baking powder. Beat flour mixture into creamed mixture. Set aside.
- To make topping, mix together sugars, cinnamon and flour.
- Cut butter in sugar mixture until mixture resembles coarse crumbs.
- Stir in pecans. Spread half of cake batter into greased and floured 9″ x 13″ pan. Sprinkle with half of topping mixture.
- Repeat with other half of batter ending with topping. Bake at 350 degrees 45 minutes.
- Serves 16-24.

High Altitude Adjustments:
- 5,000 feet: Decrease sugar by 2 tbsp in cake portion. Increase flour by 2 tbsp. Topping does not need adjustment.
- 8,000 feet and over: Decrease sugar by 3 tbsp in cake portion. Increase flour by 3 tbsp. Add 1 tbsp milk. May want to increase oven temperature to 375 degrees. Topping does not need adjustment.

A VISIT TO THE WESTERN SLOPE

Early explorers dubbed Western Colorado "Standing Up Country," because of the rugged mountains that seemingly rise straight up from the banks of the roaring rivers below. Grand Junction is the largest city on Colorado's Western Slope. Located 4,600 feet above sea level in the Grand Valley at the junction of the Colorado and Gunnison Rivers, its dry, mild climate has prompted the nickname "Banana Belt of Colorado."

Just outside Grand Junction stands Grand Mesa, the world's largest flat-top mountain. The black-green tableland rises 10,500 feet on crimson cliffs standing on end like the pages of a book, prompting early viewers to name them "bookcliffs." The valley below is lush with fruit orchards. The quaint town of Palisade, at the base of the Mesa, was once dubbed "The Peach Capital of the World."

Cola Date Loaf

1¼ cups Coca-Cola
1 (8 oz) pkg pitted, chopped dates
1 cup packed brown sugar
2 tbsp vegetable oil
2 cups Horizon All-Purpose Flour
1 tsp baking soda
1 tsp baking powder
1 tsp cinnamon
1 tsp finely grated lemon peel
1 egg
1 tsp vanilla or coffee extract
½ cup chopped Mrs. Sutler's Pecans

- Heat cola to boiling.
- Remove from heat and stir in dates, mixing very well.
- Stir in brown sugar and oil. Set aside to cool.
- Stir together flour, baking soda, baking powder, cinnamon and lemon peel.
- Add to cola mixture, along with egg, extract and nuts.
- Spoon batter into generously greased 9" x 5" loaf pan.
- Bake at 350 degrees 1 hour, or until cake tests done. Cool on rack 20 minutes.
- Remove from pan and wrap.
- Store overnight before slicing.
- Makes 1 loaf.

Apple Bread

1 cup GW Granulated Sugar
1 cup GW Brown Sugar
3 eggs, beaten
1 cup vegetable oil
2 cups diced Colorado Apples
1 tbsp vanilla
3 cups Hungarian® All-Purpose Flour
1 tsp salt
¼ tsp baking powder
1 tbsp cinnamon
1 tsp baking soda
1 tsp nutmeg
½ cup chopped Bennett Walnuts
(optional)

- Combine sugars and eggs.
- Add oil, apples and vanilla. Add dry ingredients to creamed mixture. Blend well.
- Stir in walnuts, if desired.
- Pour into 2, 8" x 4" loaf pans.
- Bake at 350 degrees 50-60 minutes.
- Makes 2 loaves.

Colorado Peach Bread

½ cup Rocky Mountain Butter
1 cup Holly Granulated Sugar
3 eggs
1¾ cups Hungarian® All-Purpose Flour
1½ tsp baking powder
1 tsp salt
½ tsp baking soda
1 tsp cinnamon
2 cups coarsely chopped, fresh
Go for Go-Bo Peaches
3 tbsp frozen orange juice concentrate,
thawed and undiluted
1 tsp vanilla
½ cup chopped Bennett Pecans
(optional)

- Cream butter; gradually add sugar, beating well.
- Add eggs, 1 at a time, beating well after each addition.
- Combine flour, baking powder, salt, baking soda and cinnamon; add to creamed mixture alternately with peaches, beginning and ending with flour mixture.
- Stir in orange juice, vanilla and pecans, if desired.
- Pour batter into greased and floured 9" x 5" x 3" loaf pan.
- Bake at 350 degrees 1 hour, or until wooden toothpick comes out clean.
- Cool in pan 10 minutes; remove from pan and cool completely.
- Serves 10-12.

COAL MINE UTOPIA

John C. Osgood brought himself and an idea to the Colorado coal fields in the early 1880s. As part of his coal empire he built an "ideal" industrial community for the workers in his coal mines. They were provided with attractive homes and a modern community with library, theatre, inn and many other comforts, all in the town of Redstone, which Osgood created. He even built a spectacular forty-two room manor house, Cleverholm, for himself. But his vision only lasted for a decade, until Osgood lost control of his mine and the community fell into disrepair. Another tale of the Colorado mountains.

Snow Capped Blueberry Sour Cream Bread

2⅓ cups Wheat Land Farms All-Purpose Flour

1½ tsp baking powder

½ tsp baking soda

¾ cup Holly Granulated Sugar

⅓ cup Meadow Gold Sour Cream

¼ cup vegetable oil

1½ tsp cinnamon

2 tsp vanilla

3 eggs

½ cup chopped Bennett Pecans or Almonds

1 cup frozen blueberries or 1 (10 oz) pkg frozen strawberries, chopped

Glaze:

½ cup Holly Powdered Sugar

2 tsp Meadow Gold Sour Cream

⅛ tsp vanilla

1 tsp water

- Preheat oven to 350 degrees.
- Grease and flour sides of 9″ x 5″ x 3″ loaf pan; place waxed paper in bottom of pan.
- Beat flour, baking powder, baking soda, sugar, sour cream, oil, cinnamon, vanilla and eggs 50 strokes.
- Stir in pecans or almonds and berries. Pour into pan. Bake 55 minutes, or until wooden toothpick inserted in center comes out clean.
- Cool 5 minutes; remove from pan. Cool completely on wire rack.
- To glaze, mix powdered sugar, sour cream and vanilla. Stir in water until smooth and of desired consistency.
- Serves 10-12.

ROLE OF THE PINON NUT

Some experts believe that the tiny nuts of pinion pine trees actually made it possible for the inhabitants of the cliff dwellings near Mesa Verde in southwestern Colorado to evolve into an agricultural society. Besides their own value as food, the nuts may have been traded with tribes farther south for corn, beans and squash. They can be eaten raw, roasted or boiled. Some tribes are said to have smashed the nuts into a paste, similar to peanut butter or almond paste, which they used to spread on hot corn cakes. Today, pinon nuts are still a favorite delicacy of the southwest. They are used in breads, muffins, cookies, cakes, salads, sauces, dressings, candies and a variety of side dishes.

Honey Bran Muffins

1 cup all-purpose flour
1 cup all-bran cereal
½ tsp baking soda
½ tsp salt (optional)
2½ tsp baking powder
¾ cup Meadow Gold Old Style Buttermilk
1 egg
¼ cup vegetable oil
¼ cup Honeyville Whipped Cinnamon, Raspberry or Apricot HoneySpread
honey and butter

- Combine dry ingredients in bowl. Make well in center.
- Combine buttermilk, egg, oil and honey spread.
- Add to dry ingredients and stir.
- Pour into muffin tins; bake in 375 degree oven 20 minutes.
- Serve warm with honey and butter.
- Makes 12 muffins.

High Altitude Adjustments:

- 5,000 feet: Increase flour by 2 tbsp. Decrease baking powder to 1 tsp. Decrease sugar by 1 tbsp.
- 8,000 feet and above: Increase flour by 3 tbsp. Decrease baking powder to 1 tsp. Decrease sugar by 1 tbsp. Add 2 tbsp milk. May want to increase oven temperature to 375 degrees.

MOUNTAIN MUSIC

Music is an integral part of Colorado. The settlers brought music with them when they arrived, and it has flourished ever since. Festivals abound during summer months, attracting acclaimed artists as well as visitors who have heard the praises of these get-togethers in Aspen, Breckenridge, Keystone, Telluride and Vail, to name just a few. What could be more envigorating than to sit in the cool Rocky Mountain air on a moonlight night and listen to a favorite concerto by Mozart or a mournful tune by Hank Williams or something cool and low by a favorite jazz artist. And when the outdoor festivals end and winter begins, the Colorado Symphony Orchestra, the Denver Chamber Orchestra and a variety of other artists will perform throughout the state.

Molly Brown's Breakfast Muffins

3 cups sifted Hungarian®
All-Purpose Flour
4 tsp baking powder
½ cup Holly Granulated Sugar
½ tsp salt
1 tsp cinnamon
½ cup raisins
2 eggs, beaten
¼ cup melted Meadow Gold Butter
1 cup Meadow Gold Milk

- Preheat oven to 350 degrees.
- Sift dry ingredients together; mix in raisins.
- Mix beaten eggs, butter and milk together.
- Combine mixtures and stir gently, just enough to dampen flour. Allow mixture to stand 15-30 minutes.
- Fill muffin tins ⅔ full and bake 20 minutes.
- Makes 15 muffins.

High Altitude Adjustments:
- 5,000 feet: Add 2 tbsp flour. Decrease baking powder to 3 tsp. Reduce sugar by 2 tbsp.
- 8,000 feet and over: Add 3 tbsp flour. Decrease baking powder to 2¾ tsp. Reduce sugar by 3 tbsp.

GETTING USED TO GRANDEUR

The one thing that strikes people about Colorado is the size. Not just the height of mountains, but the space that surrounds you. In many areas of the state, the nearest store is miles away. First-time visitors may become a bit frustrated initially, but in time the vastness of it all becomes an attribute. Towns are not piled on top of towns, nor buildings upon buildings. Separation exists, and time to consider what you are seeing. As Zebulon Pike discovered after first seeing Pikes Peak, it was not nearly as close as he thought.

Sausage Bread

1 loaf Italian bread dough
1-1½ lbs Canino's Italian Rope Sausage
1 (16 oz) ctn ricotta cheese
1 tbsp Colorado Spice Co. Parsley
¾ tsp grated Romano cheese
6 eggs
melted butter

- Preheat oven to 400 degrees.
- Lightly oil bottom and sides of 13" x 9" x 2" glass baking dish.
- Roll or stretch part of dough to cover bottom and sides of pan. Reserve enough dough to cover top.
- Cook sausage until there is no pink.
- To make filling, mix ricotta cheese, parsley and Romano cheese.
- In separate bowl, whisk or mix together eggs.
- Cut sausage into 2" pieces; place on top of dough in pan.
- Pour ricotta cheese mixture evenly over sausage layer in baking dish; then pour eggs on top.
- Stretch or roll remaining dough to cover dish; seal edges.
- Reduce heat to 350 degrees and bake 1 hour, or until medium brown.
- Once bread is out of oven, brush top lightly with melted butter and cover bread with a cloth.
- Serve hot or cold.
- Serves 16-24.

BEVERAGES

The beauty of Steamboat Springs

Photo by Gerald Brimacombe

A WORLD OF SOOTHING SILENCE

Silence, that may be the first thing you hear. If that sounds strange think about the last time you actually heard silence, or even attempted to do so. But it does not take long to begin to hear the silence once you have entered the world of Colorado's high country. It's a place where even the smallest thoughts are brushed away, and you can steep yourself in quietude. It may have been high country silence that attracted some to the state. And it certainly is a reason why people stay.

Mint Smoothie

2 cups boiling water

*8 Celestial Seasonings Mint Magic®
Herb Tea Bags*

½ cup chocolate syrup

4 cups Graves Dairy Milk

whipped cream (optional)

- Pour boiling water over tea bags and steep 5 minutes; remove tea bags.
- Add chocolate syrup to hot tea.
- Stir in milk.
- Heat to serving temperature. Do not boil.
- Serve with dollop of whipped cream, if desired.
- Serves 6-8.

Sunny Orchard

4 cups boiling water

*8 Celestial Seasonings Country Peach
Spice® Herb Tea Bags*

4 cups Skyland Apple Juice

cinnamon sticks (optional)

- Pour boiling water over tea bags and steep 5 minutes; remove tea bags.
- Stir in juice.
- Heat to serving temperature. Do not boil.
- Pour into serving cups with optional cinnamon stick stirrers.
- Serves 6-8.

Zinger® Slush

1 cup boiling water
8 Celestial Seasonings Orange Zinger®
Tea Bags
1 cup cold Deep Rock Artesian Water
2-3 cups crushed ice
1 pt Meadow Gold Orange Sherbet

- Pour boiling water over tea bags and steep 5 minutes; remove tea bags.
- Pour tea, cold water, ice and sherbet into blender; blend until slushy.
- Serves 4.

Peach Shake

2 cups Colorado Peaches
1¼ cups half and half
1½ cups Golden Peaks Milk
¼ cup sugar or honey
1¼ tsp vanilla
½ tsp brandy flavoring

- Place all ingredients in blender; blend on high until smooth.
- Serve immediately.
- Serves 4.

Cafe Mexicano

¼ cup Golden Peaks Heavy Cream
¾ tsp Colorado Spice Co. Cinnamon, divided
¼ tsp Colorado Spice Co. Nutmeg
1 tbsp sugar
4 tsp chocolate syrup
2½ cups brewed double strength hot Boyer's Coffee

- Whip cream with ¼ tsp cinnamon; add nutmeg and sugar. Whip until cream just holds its peaks.
- Put 1 tsp chocolate syrup into each of 4 demitasse cups.
- Stir remaining cinnamon into coffee and pour into cups.
- Stir well to blend in syrup.
- Spoon whipped cream on top.
- Serves 4.

THE CHILLY TOWN OF FRASER

Although most of Colorado's weather is exceptionally nice the year around, Fraser, Colorado, is a different story. Temperatures remain low even in the summer. Situated near a highly popular skiing area, Fraser amazes even the long-time residents of the state with its low readings. It even vied with other terribly cold areas in the northern U.S. for the dubious title of "Icebox of the Nation." The results were not totally conclusive, but Fraser along with International Falls, Minnesota were declared the two coldest areas in the nation.

Hot Cranberry-Apple Snap

2 cups boiling water
8 Celestial Seasonings Cranberry Cove®
Herb Tea Bags
4 cups Skyland Apple Juice
orange slices

- Pour boiling water over tea bags and steep 5 minutes; remove tea bags.
- Stir in apple juice.
- Heat to serving temperature. Do not boil.
- Float orange slices on top.
- Serves 6-8.

Mulled Wine

2 (750 ml) btls Pikes Peak Vineyards
Colorado Red Wine
⅔ cup water
1 ctn Aspen Mulling Spices

- Mix all ingredients together; serve hot or cold.
- To serve hot, gently heat mixed ingredients until very warm.
- Serves 6-8.

Berry Apple Bliss

2 cups boiling water

8 Celestial Seasonings Wild Forest Blackberry® Herb Tea Bags

2 cups Mountain Sun Apple Juice

2 cups cold water

4 cups ice cubes

2 (12 oz) cans Canada Dry Lemon/Lime Seltzer

ice

- Pour boiling water over tea bags and steep 5 minutes; remove tea bags.
- Add apple juice, cold water, ice and lemon/lime seltzer.
- Serve over ice.
- Serves 11-14.

Spiced Cranapple Brew

2 tbsp Simmers & Seasonings Mulling Spice Mix

1 gal cranapple juice

- Tie spice mix in muslin bag.
- Gently simmer cranapple juice and spice mix 30 minutes or more.
- Serves 16.

The Grand Mesa

2 oz Grand Marnier

3 oz Colorado Crystal Original

lemon twist to garnish

- Pour liquids over ice; stir.
- Garnish with lemon twist.
- Serves 1.

MELON COUNTRY

To folks in this part of the country, the town of Rocky Ford is to melons what Sunkist is to oranges. In the late 1880's this hamlet in eastern Colorado, about 175 miles southeast of Denver, became the nation's first commercial cantaloupe center. Shipped from Colorado to major population centers such as Kansas City, Chicago and New York City, the yellow melons quickly gained a reputation for their sweet, succulent flavor. Today, seed production is a mainstay of the area. Produce, grass and flower seeds also are shipped throughout the country from this tiny town, whose population and elevation figures are about equal, slightly over 4,000.

Because of the exceptional quality of the area's melons and pioneering efforts in shipping, Rocky Ford long ago earned the title "Melon Capital of the World." Melon Day is celebrated every August.

Wild Almond

1½ oz Amaretto

5 oz Colorado Crystal Wild Mountain Cherry

cherry to garnish

- Pour liquids over ice; stir.
- Garnish with cherry.
- Serves 1.

Hot Spiced Wine

4 cups Deep Rock Artesian Water

1 cup GW Granulated Sugar

18 whole cloves

¼ rind of lemon

⅛ tsp All American Seasonings Allspice

1 (750 ml) btl Pikes Peak Vineyards Colorado Red Wine

8 cinnamon sticks (optional)

- Boil ingredients, except wine and cinnamon sticks, 15 minutes.
- Strain out solids.
- Add wine and warm, but do not boil.
- Serve with optional cinnamon stick stirrers.
- Serves 8.

Raspberry Swirl

1 cup boiling water

6 Celestial Seasonings Raspberry Patch® Herb Tea Bags

½ cup ice cubes

½ cup cold water

1 pt Meadow Gold Raspberry Sherbet

1½ cups Canada Dry Club Soda

Meadow Gold Vanilla Ice Cream

- Pour boiling water over tea bags in 2 cup container and steep 5 minutes; remove tea bags.
- Add ice to hot tea; stir until melted and add cold water.
- Whirl with raspberry sherbet in blender.
- Divide among 6 glasses and add club soda; stir.
- Serve with scoop of vanilla ice cream.
- Serves 6.

Telluride Luau

1½ oz vodka

2 oz pineapple juice

3 oz Colorado Crystal Lemon

lemon twist to garnish

- Pour liquids over ice; stir.
- Garnish with lemon twist.
- Serves 1.

Capuccino Cooler

1 cup brewed extra strength Boyer's French Roast Coffee, at room temperature

1 cup Robinson Milk

2 small scoops Jackson Coffee Ice Cream

¼ cup brandy or bourbon

dash vanilla

nutmeg

- In small bowl, stir coffee and milk; blend well.
- Pour into blender; add ice cream, brandy or bourbon and vanilla. Blend until smooth and frothy.
- Pour into 2 tall glasses. Sprinkle with nutmeg.
- Serve immediately.
- Serves 2.

SOUPS, STEWS & CHILI

Winter roundup

Photo by Larry Pierce

WHEN BRECKENRIDGE GOT "LOST"

Visitors to Breckenridge, Colorado, may not know they are actually in a foreign territory! During the mining days, the town was not a part of the United States or Colorado. When the U.S. government purchased land from the Indians, a large area was accidentally left out. It still belonged to the Indians, and Breckenridge was a part of that overlooked land. Nobody discovered this fact until 1936! At that time the Colorado Governor, Ed Johnson, welcomed the area into the state and many of the citizens rejoiced. However, Coloradans are independent folks, and none more so than the citizens of Breckenridge. They still retain the right to be an "independent kingdom" for three days every year.

Beef Stew with Italian Sausage

2 lbs Banes Beef Chuck, cut into small pieces

2 lbs Canino's Mild Italian Sausage

1 large Sun Tan Onion, diced

1 medium green bell pepper, diced

¼ cup chopped Bellwether Farms Parsley

¼ cup chopped Bellwether Farms Basil

salt and black pepper

1 (15 oz) can Diven Tomatoes, chopped

1 (6 oz) can Cream of the Valley Tomato Paste

5 large Russett Burbank Potatoes, cubed

1 cup diced celery

1 (20 oz) pkg frozen mixed vegetables

1 (16 oz) can peas, drained

1 (16 oz) can cut green beans, drained

- Brown meat, sausage, onion and bell pepper.
- Add parsley, basil, salt and pepper; brown well.
- Add tomatoes and tomato paste.
- Cook 30 minutes.
- Add remaining vegetables.
- Cook 2 hours.
- Serves 6-8.

LARIMER SQUARE

Larimer Square in Denver, site of one of the city's original encampments, is named after one of Denver's founders. During the recent past, it has gone through several transitions, but today it is a delightful enclave for shopping, dining and entertainment. Nearby sits the Tabor Center complex with its stores and hotel. Larimer Square doubles as the site for various events designed to draw shoppers. Around the holidays, the Square dresses up in holiday finery and brings in mimes, musicians, stilt walkers, bicycle riders and choral groups. A highlight of that season is the Newfoundland Dog-Cart event. Children can be taken on a ride around the area by the huge black dogs. Another feature is the annual Tuba Christmas Carol Concert. Two hundred tuba players sit in the crisp winter air and play favorite carols.

Colorado Chili

1½ lbs Maverick Ranch NaturaLite Ground Beef
1 large green pepper, diced
1 large onion, diced
1 clove garlic, minced
3 tbsp F & J Chili Powder
1 (14.5 oz) can Kuner's Peeled Tomatoes
½ cup F & J Steak Sauce
½ cup water
1 (16 oz) can pinto beans, drained
grated cheese (optional)

- In large pot, over high heat, cook beef, green pepper, onion and garlic, stirring frequently, until browned, about 15 minutes.
- Stir in chili powder; cook 1 minute.
- Drain and chop tomatoes, saving liquid.
- Add tomatoes, liquid, steak sauce and water to mixture.
- Bring to boil.
- Cover; reduce heat and simmer 45 minutes, stirring frequently.
- Stir in beans; cover and simmer 15-20 minutes.
- Cover with grated cheese, if desired.
- Serves 4-6.

FIRST SETTLERS, THE INDIANS

The first real settlers of Colorado were the Indians. They trace back to the Anasazi people who inhabitated the western part of the state around 1100 A.D. By 1300, the Ute peoples began moving in, and by 1600 they were living in the western and northwestern areas of Colorado.

About the same time, the Apache and Navajos were locating in the eastern and southern regions. By 1720 the Utes were spread throughout the state while the Comanches remained in settlements along the eastern border. By 1820, when the first fur traders and mountain men began arriving, the Utes were in the western half of the state, the Shoshoni in the very northwest tip, the Arapahoes and Cheyenne in the northeast and the eastern plains, while the Kiowa and Comanche peoples were in the southeast corner.

Beef Burgundy Stew

¾ tsp dried Colorado Spice Co. Marjoram Leaves

¾ tsp pepper

2¼ lbs boneless Banes Beef Chuck, cut into 1½" pieces

2 tbsp vegetable oil

1 (13.75 oz) can beef broth

1 cup Pikes Peak Vineyards Cabernet Sauvignon

2 cloves garlic, minced

4 medium carrots, cut into ½" pieces

½ lb Rakhra Mushrooms

½ lb pearl onions, peeled

1 tbsp cornstarch

¼ cup water

- Combine marjoram and pepper; sprinkle over beef.
- Brown beef, half at a time, in oil in Dutch oven.
- Pour off drippings.
- Add beef broth, wine and garlic; stir to combine.
- Cover tightly and simmer 1 hour.
- Add carrots and continue cooking, covered, 30 minutes.
- Add mushrooms and pearl onions; continue cooking, covered, 30 minutes.
- Combine cornstarch with water; gradually stir into stew and cook, uncovered, until thickened, 10 minutes.
- Serves 8.

SUNSET SUCCESS

Jolly Rancher Candies, known worldwide for their cellophane wrapped "Famous for Flavor" hard candies, had humble beginnings in a seventy-five-year-old farmhouse on ten acres west of Denver. In 1942, a Minneapolis airline pilot, Bill Harmsen, his wife, Dorothy, and their one year-old son, Bill Jr., left their urban surroundings and moved to the site which produced perennial fruit and flower crops. Bill continued to fly while his wife guided the farm's operations.

Hearing that the soft ice cream business was becoming lucrative, Bill gave up flying to open the first Jolly Rancher Ice Cream Store in nearby Golden in 1949. The name was their own creation, which they copyrighted, to present a friendly western image. They soon learned that the stories of huge profits in the business were mere rumors. In order to make any money at all, they had to create a new plan. They soon added a line of high quality bulk and boxed chocolates. The store's business grew and expanded to franchised candy and ice cream shops in Colorado, Wyoming and Nebraska.

Western Stew

1 lb Banes Ground Beef
salt, pepper, savory salt and garlic salt
1 large onion, diced
1 cup diced celery
4 cups cooked Red Bird Brand Pinto Beans
1 (16 oz) can whole kernel corn
2 cups chopped Top Quality Tomatoes
5 medium Inch By Inch Carrots, sliced and cooked

- Shape ground beef into small balls.
- Season with salt, pepper, savory salt and garlic salt totaste.
- Broil until brown.
- Add onion, celery, pinto beans, corn, tomatoes and carrots.
- Cook until vegetables are tender.
- Serves 5-6.

ROOM WITH A VIEW

It sits high above Interstate Highway 70, west of Denver. It is called The Clamshell House because, well, it looks like a clamshell sitting on top of a fence post. It really is not a house, rather it is the shell of a house, empty inside, but with views of one hundred or more miles in any direction. If you want to move in you would have to spend plenty of time and money putting in all the creature comforts. Designed originally as an experiment by the developer, the house now rates as artwork. There is nothing constructed like it anywhere else in the world.

As you drive the stretch of highway below it, you may see people pointing or hanging out the windows of their cars to see the house. Should you move in you would be truly isolated up there. Oh yes, the Clamshell House has been for sale for some time. So, if you would like an isolated room with a view it might be right for you.

Chili with Italian Sausage

2 lbs Coleman Natural Beef Ground Chili Beef

2 lbs Canino's Italian Sausage

1 large Sun Tan Onion, diced

salt to taste

1 tsp black pepper

⅓ cup Sequoyah House San Juan Chili Seasoning

1 tsp cumin

1 (6 oz) can Cream of the Valley Tomato Paste

water

3 (16 oz) cans pinto beans, drained

- Brown beef, sausage and onion.
- Add salt, pepper, chili seasoning and cumin.
- Add tomato paste with enough water to cover meat.
- Cook for 30 minutes.
- Add beans.
- Simmer for 2 hours.
- Serves 8-10.

Beef Stew

2 tbsp Dixon & Sons Q-Mix
2 lbs Coleman Natural Beef Stew Meat
1 cup diced celery
¾ cup sliced carrots
1 small Banner Onion, diced
2 large Martins Leader Potatoes, chopped
1 (16 oz) can Diven Tomatoes

- Sprinkle Q-Mix on meat.
- Add celery, carrots, onion, potatoes and tomatoes.
- Simmer until done.
- Serves 4.

Spicy Chili

2 strips bacon
2 lbs beef chuck, diced
2 (12 oz) cans Coors Beer
2 tbsp chili powder
1 tbsp crushed oregano
1 tbsp cumin
½ tsp cayenne
2 tsp Worcestershire sauce
1 tsp salt
1 tbsp corn meal or masa harina
¼ cup water
4 cups cooked pinto beans

- In large saucepan, cook bacon until crisp.
- Drain; reserve drippings in pan.
- Crumble bacon; set aside.
- In drippings, brown meat.
- Add next 7 ingredients.
- Bring to boil; reduce heat.
- Simmer, covered, 45 minutes.
- Combine corn meal and water; stir into hot mixture.
- Add crumbled bacon; return to boil.
- Reduce heat; simmer, covered, 15 minutes.
- Serve with beans.
- Serves 8.

©Meredith Corporation 1981.

Maroon Bells near Aspen

Photo by Jeff Andrew

MOUNTAIN BUILDING

How did all this beauty that is Colorado's Rockies begin? Geologists say that about 275 million years ago the last great range of mountains to stand before today's Rockies was being eroded away to its base. These have been called the Ancestral Rockies. About 70 million years ago the Rockies we know emerged. As the mountains rose, the fast-driving rivers took away soft sediment and moved it onto the eastern plains. The last intense period of mountain building raised the Front Range—5 to 7 million years ago, followed by the incumbent erosion. Of course, much more recent occurrences, such as the change in the earth's climate and formation of the Ice Age, have also left their mark on these majestic mountains.

Chili Con Carne

1½ lbs Banes Ground Beef
3 medium onions, chopped
1 clove garlic, finely chopped
3 tbsp shortening
4 cups cooked Pantry Pinto Beans
1 (28 oz) can Diven Tomatoes
3 bay leaves
1 tbsp salt
4 dried chili peppers
2-3 tbsp F & J Chili Powder
water

- Fry meat, onions and garlic in shortening, stirring until browned.
- Add remaining ingredients, including water, as needed; cover and simmer 1 hour.
- Serves 6-8.

PRUNES

His name was Prunes, and he was extraordinary. If he had been human, he would have been awarded a comfortable pension, and he would have received a pat on the back for his years of service. However, Prunes was a burro. Not just any burro, he became the symbol for all of the burros who labored so long and hard in and around the mines. He served faithfully for fifty years. Burros were essential in the mines. They brought in provisions and took out the ore. In some areas, if it were not for the burros, the ore might still be in those mines. Prunes is buried in Fairplay where a monument adorned with his four last horseshoes and halter, is dedicated to him for a job well done.

Old-Fashioned Hot Dog Chowder

1 (10.75 oz) can vegetable soup
1 (11 oz) can hot dog bean soup
1 soup can Busch® Beer
1 soup can water
3 slices Orowheat Rye Bread, cut into ½" cubes
¼ cup Rocky Mountain Butter

- Heat together soups, beer and water.
- Sauté bread cubes in butter until crisp and golden.
- Spoon soup into bowls.
- Sprinkle with rye bread croutons.
- Serves 6.

Pea Soup

1 (4 oz) env dehydrated pea soup
1 cup Budweiser® Beer
2 cups water
1 tbsp instant minced onion
4 cooked European Sausage Bratwurst, Breakfast or Polish Sausages, thinly sliced

- Make soup according to pkg directions using beer, water and onion.
- Simmer as directed until soup is slightly thickened.
- Add sausages and simmer 5 minutes.
- Serves 4.

LONG BIKE RIDE

Colorado's recreational attractions are expanding to meet the interests of an ever-growing and changing population. Kokopelli's Trail is one example. It's a 128-mile mountain bike trail, located between Grand Junction and Moab, Utah. The Bureau of Land Management and a small group of volunteers worked hard to "put it on the map." The project lasted approximately six months from conception to reality in early 1989.

The trail consists of existing jeep roads, which remain open to motorized vehicles, and eleven miles of single-track trail which the group built by hand. The trail association hopes to eventually add trails that will unite the communities of the Colorado Plateau, from Aspen to Zion National Park in Utah, Chaco Canyon in New Mexico and Park City, Utah.

Grandma BJ's French Market Soup

1 pkg Moki Bean Soup Mix
8 cups water
2 ham hocks
salt and pepper
1 (16 oz) can Diven Tomatoes, strained and chopped
1 large onion, chopped
1 clove garlic, minced
1-1½ tsp Colorado Spice Co. Chili Powder
or
1 chili pepper, chopped
½ lemon, juiced

- Rinse beans.
- Cover with water 2" above beans; soak overnight.
- Drain beans; add water, ham hocks, salt and pepper.
- Cover and bring to boil.
- Reduce heat; simmer 2 hours, or until beans are tender.
- Add remaining ingredients; stirring occasionally.
- Remove ham from bone and return to soup.
- Serves 6-8.

HOT AIR BALLOONING

The colorful balloons rising against magnificent Colorado scenery have become popular subjects for photographers and artists. Several Colorado communities have begun hosting annual balloon festivals during the summer months. Among those cities that stage events are Grand Junction, Telluride, Carbondale, LaVeta, Montrose, Gunnison, Snowmass, Steamboat Springs, Castle Rock, Avon, Colorado Springs and Fort Collins. The events are usually held from the beginning of June to mid-September. If you plan to attend, bring a camera.

Chilled Shrimp Bisque

1½ lbs Keeton Fisheries Shrimp, peeled, deveined and cooked

2 cups Mountain High® Plain Yoghurt

1½ cups water

2 tsp Dijon mustard

¾ tsp onion salt

¼ tsp white pepper

½ cup finely shredded Piedmont Farms Cucumber

- Reserve ½ cup cooked shrimp; coarsely chop remaining shrimp.
- In blender or food processor, combine all ingredients except reserved shrimp and cucumber.
- Blend until smooth.
- In bowl, combine shrimp mixture and cucumber.
- Cover; chill 2-4 hours to blend flavors.
- Garnish with reserved shrimp.
- Serves 4.

Cioppino

1 (8 oz) btl clam juice

½ cup Carlson Vineyards White Riesling

1 (15 oz) ctn Chapin's Supreme Pepperonata Sauce

½ lb firm white fish, flaked

½ lb assorted shell fish, removed from shell

Schmidt's French Bread

- In saucepan, stir clam juice and wine into pepperonata sauce.
- Add fish; simmer until fish is cooked.
- Serve with bread.
- Serves 4.

Black Bean Chili

¼ *cup vegetable oil*
1 onion, chopped
1 (16 oz) can Mile High Tomatoes
2¼ tsp cumin
2¼ tsp oregano
1½ tsp paprika
¼ tsp cayenne
1½ tsp chili powder
2 cloves garlic, minced
4 tsp canned chopped green chilies
1 (11 oz) pkg Mitie Mixes Black Beans
1 bay leaf
4 cups water
2-2½ cups Bar-S Monterey Jack Cheese, divided
4-5 tbsp Meadow Gold Sour Cream

- Heat salad oil in large pot.
- Sauté onion.
- Add tomatoes, spices, garlic and green chilies.
- Simmer 15 minutes.
- Sort and wash black beans; add to pot with bay leaf and water.
- Bring to boil; simmer 2½ hours, or until tender.
- Add water, if needed, to keep beans covered.
- Before serving, put ½ cup grated cheese into each bowl.
- Pour chili into bowls; top with dollop of sour cream.
- Serves 4-5.

Potato Soup

1 (3 oz) env dehydrated potato soup
1 cup Michelob® Beer
2¼ cups water
¾ cup Robinson Milk
4 tbsp Robinson Butter, divided
2 cups coarsely grated Swiss cheese
croutons

- Make soup according to pkg directions using beer and water; simmer 7 minutes.
- Add milk and reheat, but do not boil.
- Spoon soup into bowls.
- Add a tbsp of butter, a generous amount of grated cheese and a few croutons to each bowl.
- Serves 4.

PHOTOS THAT LIVE

He captured Colorado on film. The photographs taken by William H. Jackson fixed the beauty and excitement of those early Colorado days in the minds of people throughout the nation, and for the generations that have followed.

In 1873, 1874 and 1875, Jackson went deep into the mountains with his camera and crew. He disregarded the dangers around him to get the best vantage point. The results were wonderful photographs that are now irreplaceable. He later opened a photographic studio in Denver, and never again produced the intense photographs of his earlier days. His pictures remain some of the best historic glimpses we have of Colorado's past.

Vegetarian Chowder

Ingredients	Instructions
1 lb Pantry Small White Navy Beans	• Sort, rinse and soak beans.
6-8 cups water	• Drain in large kettle.
1½ tsp salt	• Cook beans in 6-8 cups water with salt, until tender, about 2-2½ hours. Do not drain.
1 cup chopped onion	
1½ cups chopped celery	• Meanwhile, cook onion and celery briefly in butter in 1½ qt saucepan.
¼ cup Rocky Mountain Butter	
¼ cup Eartharvest Unbleached All-Purpose Flour	• Blend in flour, salt and pepper.
½ tsp salt	• Stir in milk, and bring mixture to boil.
⅛ tsp pepper	• Add to beans and their liquid, along with remaining ingredients.
3 cups Royal Crest Milk	
1 (16 oz) can Mile High Tomatoes	• Heat to boiling.
1 (16 oz) can whole kernel corn	• For extra zip, add dash of hot pepper sauce.
¼ lb Bar-S Foods Monterey Jack Cheese	
hot pepper sauce	• Serves 12.

THE BOULDERADO

The Hotel Boulderado. What was that again, a mix of Boulder and Colorado? Clearly. And that name is truly unique. It's chiseled above the entry to an elegant hotel in Boulder, Colorado, designed to assure visitors and meeting attendees a first class establishment in that fair city rather than driving to Denver to stay the night.

Opened in 1908 it still serves the transient visitor or conference participant. Located just off the downtown business district, it has been refurbished regularly but still holds that quaint Victorian charm and decor which it had upon opening. Its dining room is exceptionally popular with local residents and is filled to overflowing during football weekends at the University or during Commencement exercises. The restored lobby area retains the flavor of its early days and inspires a number of couples to use the large stairway landing overlooking it as a site for their weddings.

Smoked Salmon Chowder

¼ lb salt pork, no rind
1 large onion, chopped
½ cup diced celery
2 carrots, sliced
3 Hi-Dolly Potatoes, coarsely diced
2 cups water
1 bay leaf
3 cups Golden Peaks Milk
2 lbs smoked salmon, slivered
1 cup Golden Peaks Whipping Cream
salt and pepper

- Blanch salt pork in water 5 minutes; drain and cut into small cubes.
- Brown cubes in kettle.
- Add onion, celery and carrots; sauté until onion is transparent.
- Add potatoes, water, bay leaf and milk.
- Cover; simmer 10 minutes.
- Add salmon slivers and stir to distribute; simmer 5-10 minutes.
- Remove bay leaf.
- Stir in cream.
- Add salt and pepper, if desired.
- Serves 8.

SAN LUIS VALLEY: POTATO COUNTRY

Potatoes are one of Colorado's most important agricultural crops. The state ranks in the top ten producing states in the nation for all potatoes as well as summer and fall potatoes separately. Potatoes currently bring in more money than any of the state's other vegetable crops.

Colorado's primary potato growing area is the San Luis Valley located in the extreme south-central part of the state. The valley is a high-altitude desert, as elevation averages 7,600 feet above sea level. Although it receives less than ten inches of rainfall each year, the valley is blessed with rich sandy loam soil and abundant underground water supplies, allowing for extensive irrigation systems.

The superb growing conditions produce a delicious crisp potato which is good for baking, frying or prepared in a variety of other ways. San Luis growers feature Russet Burbanks, Centennial Russets and Sangre varieties.

San Luis Valley Potato Soup

4 large Russet Burbank Potatoes
2 medium onions, chopped
2 slices Bar-S Bacon, chopped
2 large stalks celery, chopped
2½ cups water
1½ tsp salt
2 tbsp butter
3 cups Royal Crest Milk

- Wash, peel and slice potatoes into large soup kettle.
- Add onions, bacon, celery and water.
- Cover and cook until potatoes are tender.
- Mash vegetables, in their liquid; add salt, butter and milk.
- Heat just to boiling, but do not boil.
- If using slow cooker, do not add milk until just before serving.
- Heat until soup is hot.
- Serves 4-5.

Cream of Curry Chicken Soup

1 (15 oz) ctn Chapin's Supreme Curry Sauce

4 cups chicken broth

1 cup diced, cooked chicken

1 cup cooked rice

1 (10 oz) pkg frozen baby peas

½ cup Meadow Gold Old Style Heavy Cream

minced green onions or honey roasted peanuts to garnish

- Combine curry sauce with chicken broth, chicken and rice.
- Add peas and simmer 15 minutes.
- Add cream and turn off heat.
- Garnish with green onions or honey roasted peanuts.
- Serves 4-6.

Gingered Carrot Soup

½ cup chopped onion

1½ tsp chopped fresh ginger
or
¾ tsp ground ginger

2 tbsp butter or margarine

4 cups pared, sliced carrots

3½ cups water

4 tsp chicken flavor instant bouillon

2 cups Mountain High® Plain Yoghurt

2 tbsp all-purpose flour

¼ tsp cinnamon

1 cup Meadow Gold Milk

- In large saucepan, cook onion and ginger in butter until tender.
- Add carrots, water and bouillon; bring to boil.
- Reduce heat; cook covered until tender.
- In blender or food processor, blend half the carrot mixture until smooth; add remaining carrot mixture and blend.
- In saucepan, combine yoghurt, flour and cinnamon; add milk and carrot puree.
- Over low heat, cook and stir until hot (do not boil).
- Garnish as desired.
- Serves 5-7.

SALADS

Bustling Streets of Boulder

Photo by Anne Krause

RISE OF GATES RUBBER

By 1914, the tread company started by Charles C. Gates and his brother, John, became International Half-Sole, producing a tread cover for automobile tires. They now made their product from rubber and fabric and cemented it in place over worn treads. The company soon moved to south Broadway in Denver, the location that would be its home for nearly seventy-five years. In 1917, John Gates made a revolutionary discovery that sent the company on an upward spiral for years to come. In his new Cole coupe, he noted V-shaped pulleys powered by rope turning the radiator fan. He decided to create a V-belt made of rubber and fabric. It was the world's first, and it became an industry standard. In 1918, the company became Gates Rubber Company, and in 1919, they introduced the first balloon tire.

Wilted Spinach Beef Salad

2 lbs Maverick Ranch NaturaLite Beef Ribeye Steaks

3 tbsp olive oil

½ cup finely sliced green onions

2 cloves garlic, finely minced

2 tbsp teriyaki sauce

2 tbsp sherry

1 tsp Dijon mustard

1 tsp horseradish

½ tsp dillweed

salt and pepper

5 cups bite-size pieces Charley Hayashida Spinach, cleaned and stems removed

1 medium red onion, thinly sliced

1 cup grated Monterey Jack cheese

8 Life Force Cherry Tomatoes, halved

- Cut steaks into thin strips, approximately 1½"-2" long and ⅛" thick.
- Heat olive oil in large frying pan over medium heat; add onion and garlic and fry 1-2 minutes.
- Add beef strips; stir-fry over high heat 2-3 minutes.
- Mix together teriyaki sauce, sherry, mustard, horseradish and dillweed.
- Add to beef in skillet, cook 1 minute.
- Season with salt and pepper to taste.
- In large salad bowl, place spinach, onion, cheese and tomatoes. Pour warm beef and sauce over spinach mixture. Toss to coat.
- Serve immediately.
- Serves 6-8.

MORE GATES INNOVATIONS

By 1927, the Gates Rubber Company of Denver had become one of the most innovative in the industry. New creations included the rubber hose, the first steam hose for locomotives, the garden hose and the automobile radiator hose. The company survived the Great Depression because of its wide product base. In 1931, heavy duty V-belts replaced chain and gear drives. During World War II, Gates supplied the war effort with over one thousand products. In the 1950s and 1960s they expanded and diversified considerably, and took on such enterprises as cattle ranching, a guest ranch, mutual funds management, residential land development, rechargeable lead-acid batteries, and executive jet aircraft (Gates Learjet). The company is still wholly owned by the Gates family.

Southwestern Pork Salad

2 cups cooked Colorado Pork, cut into slices

1 (16 oz) can kidney, pinto or garbanzo beans, drained and rinsed

1 (6 oz) can pitted black olives, drained

½ cup chopped onion

½ cup chopped Rosey Farms Green Bell Pepper

1 large Rosey Farms Tomato, peeled and chopped

2 tbsp sugar

¼ cup cider vinegar

¼ cup vegetable oil

½ tsp Colorado Spice Co. Dry Mustard

½ tsp Colorado Spice Co. Cumin

½ tsp Colorado Spice Co. Oregano

½ tsp salt

2 tbsp chopped parsley

- Mix pork, beans, olives, onion, green pepper and tomato in large bowl.
- Combine remaining ingredients in jar; shake to mix.
- Pour over pork mixture, toss and refrigerate several hours, stirring occasionally.
- Serves 6.

CATTLE FEEDING

Cattle feeding has become big business in Colorado. The business arose near the area where sugar beets are grown. Cattle are able to eat the remains of sugar production, thus making use of an otherwise waste product.

From those humble beginnings emerged one of the largest cattle feeding operations in the world, Monfort of Colorado. This giant received its start on an eighty-acre farm near Greeley, Colorado. The company buys one-year old cattle from within the region, feeds them such things as the sugar beet remains and corn, then ships them to meat packers who serve both Colorado, the Midwest and Eastern markets.

Colorado Beef Salad

¼ cup olive oil

¼ cup Marquest Orange Juice

¼ cup white wine vinegar

1 tbsp Mady's Zesty Honey Mustard

1 tbsp Lucky Clover Honey

1 tsp salt

1 tsp snipped Bellwether Farms Mint Leaves

1½ lbs cooked Colorado Beef, cut into thin strips

1 medium red onion, thinly sliced and separated into rings

romaine lettuce leaves

3 medium oranges, peeled and cut into slices

1 large avocado, peeled, seeded and sliced

- To make marinade, combine first 7 ingredients.
- Place beef strips and onion rings in glass bowl; add ½ cup marinade, stirring lightly to coat.
- Cover bowl and refrigerate 2-3 hours.
- Line serving platter with romaine; place beef and onion rings in center.
- Arrange orange and avocado slices around beef strips.
- Drizzle remaining dressing over salad.
- Serves 6.

TOP TEN IN AGRICULTURE

According to some of the most recent statistics, Colorado agriculture ranks within the top ten producing states for twenty-nine commodities. The average size of farms and ranches in the state is over 1,200 acres. Livestock and livestock products generate the largest amount of cash; cattle and calves top the list.

Colorado's total farm and food sector (all firms involved in the production, marketing and sale of food) is estimated to generate over eight percent of the state's total income.

Beef and Pasta Salad

½ lb cooked Colorado Beef Top Round Steak, thinly sliced

2 tbsp Little Chalet Dressing

2 tsp chopped parsley

1½ cups cooked Pasta Pasta Pasta Vermicelli, rinsed and drained

1 small Top Quality Tomato

1 green onion, thinly sliced

parsley to garnish

- Combine beef, salad dressing and parsley, tossing lightly to coat. Cover bowl tightly and refrigerate overnight.

- To serve, place an equal amount of vermicelli on 2 dinner plates.

- Arrange an equal amount of beef strips in spoke fashion on vermicelli.

- Cut tomato into thin slices; cut each slice in half.

- Arrange tomato slices on beef; sprinkle with onion.

- Garnish with parsley, if desired.

- Serves 2.

ANIMAL KINGDOM

"I looked out the window and what did I see, a mule deer standing there staring at me!" That little rhyme, spoken by a modern Colorado child, may best sum up why many children so love the state. Those fortunate enough to live in the foothill or mountain communities still ask wide-eyed about bobcats, mountain lions, bears, snakes and other animals, all of which they may encounter on any given day. And, of course, there are deer aplenty. Within the boundaries of many towns, as well as the more rural areas, you can awaken to find several deer in your own backyard. Homeowners may be frazzled by the deer's consumption of their flowers and plants, but the children, well, they see something much different.

Oriental Mushroom and Chicken Salad

2 tbsp slivered almonds, toasted

12 oz Rakhra Mushrooms

⅔ cup Marquest Orange Juice

⅓ cup vegetable oil

½ tsp salt

¼ tsp ginger

¼ tsp garlic powder

1 tbsp soy sauce

1 tbsp dry sherry

1 cup cooked Banes Chicken, cut into 1" cubes

1 cup cooked rice

⅓ cup diced Golden West Green Bell Pepper

2 tbsp sliced green onions

lettuce leaves (optional)

- To toast almonds, place on baking sheet in preheated 350 degree oven until light brown, 5 minutes.

- Rinse, pat dry and slice mushrooms; set aside.

- Combine orange juice, oil, salt, ginger, garlic powder, soy sauce and sherry; set aside.

- In large bowl, combine chicken, rice, green pepper, almonds, green onions and mushrooms.

- Add dressing and toss to mix.

- Cover and refrigerate at least 2 hours or overnight. Serve on bed of lettuce leaves, if desired.

- Serves 6.

TO CALIFORNIA BY BOAT?

Breckenridge, Colorado. Slips right off the tongue doesn't it? A ski town today, Breckenridge was a gold-mining area for many years, but claimed a few other distinctions as well. For example, Breckenridge had the only navy in Colorado. In the state's infancy it was believed a water-way connection existed between the Rockies and California. A colorful Breckenridge character, Sam Adams, set out to establish a navy, financed by the citizens, and dedicated to finding that waterway. The town was supportive, providing him with funds and a banner for his California-bound boats. So, in 1869, after a rousing send-off, Sam set sail on the Blue River with four flat-boats and ten seamen. However, it was not long before the boats were badly battered, and the seamen had jumped ship. The enterprise was abandoned. Sam Adams returned to Breckenridge a sadder, but wiser man.

Spicy Chicken Peanut Salad

4 cups Life Force Foods Spicy Sprouts
5 cups cooked shredded Red Bird Fryer Chicken
2 tbsp chopped green onion
½ cup chopped peanuts

Dressing:
3 tbsp peanut butter
5 tbsp vegetable oil
¼ cup soy sauce
¼ cup GW Granulated Sugar
4 tsp vinegar
1 tbsp Chinese sesame oil concentrate
½ tsp Colorado Spice Co. Cayenne

- In blender, whirl all dressing ingredients together and store in refrigerator until ready to use.
- Spread sprouts on platter.
- Top evenly with chicken.
- Sprinkle onions and peanuts on top; drizzle dressing to cover.
- Serves 4-6.

SHOPPING FOR SMALL FRY

One of the exhibits at the Denver Children's Museum that always draws the biggest crowds is the child-sized version of a grocery store. Filled with plastic roasts, empty but very realistic milk cartons, plus a melange of boxes and cans just like you would find in your local store, this exhibit has a waiting line of children ready to shop the aisles, check out, then return everything and begin again.

Besides the exhibits, the Museum regularly presents performances in its theatre directed at its young audience. Puppet shows, magic acts, even specially prepared singing and dancing routines are featured.

Once you leave the building there is still plenty to do in the outside recreational areas, including swings, walking a maze of wood beams, teeter-totters, slides and a few "special" attractions all set against the backdrop of Denver's nearby, downtown skyline.

Pinto Bean Combination Salad

1 (6 oz) pkg lemon or lime gelatin
3 tbsp vinegar
½ tsp Colorado Spice Co. Salt
2 dashes Accent
¼ cup chopped pimento
2 cups cooked Red Bird Brand Pinto Beans
¼ cup chopped Thomas Produce Green Bell Pepper
1 tbsp minced onion
2 medium Thomas Produce Tomatoes, peeled and sliced
lettuce leaves
stuffed olives, salad dressing or paprika to garnish

- Prepare gelatin according to pkg directions, using vinegar as part of liquid, add salt and Accent. Set aside to cool.
- Place small piece of pimento in center of individual molds or several pieces in bottom of large mold.
- Add enough pinto beans to cover bottom.
- Sprinkle green peppers and onion over beans.
- Add remaining beans, top with tomato slices.
- Pour cooled gelatin mixture over ingredients until tomato slices are covered. Chill until firm.
- Unmold on lettuce leaves and add garnishes.
- Serves 4-6.

PINTO BEAN COUNTRY

Down in southwestern Colorado, near the four corners area (where Colorado, Utah, Arizona and New Mexico's borders come together) pinto beans are serious words. Millions of pounds of these beans are grown in this area each year, and you can imagine what that has led to—the Pinto Bean Cooking Contest and some mighty imaginative recipes.

Let's see, how about Pinto Pizza or Pinto Bean Balls and Dip Sauce or Pinto Bean Dunkers Delight or Pinto Ice Box Cookies or…well we could go on, but you get the picture. All of these recipes and hundreds of other ones have been entered into the contest throughout the years.

For those of you not as well versed in beans, pintos are the cream-colored beans speckled in tones of light brown and especially popular in chili, refried beans and Mexican treats.

But in Cortez, Colorado, home of the Pinto Bean Cooking Contest, there are many other recipes available right now, and others just waiting to be discovered.

Nippy Pinto Bean Salad

2 cups Red Bird Brand Cooked Pinto Beans
½ cup Cream of the Valley Tomato Sauce
2 tbsp crumbled nippy cheese
1 tbsp minced onion
1 tbsp More Than Mustard Original Recipe Prepared Mustard
¼ cup minced green pepper
¼ cup minced celery
1 tbsp F & J Worcestershire Sauce
1 tbsp vinegar
6 medium Life Force Foods Tomatoes
lettuce leaves
parsley or watercress to garnish

- Mix all ingredients, except tomatoes, lettuce and garnish; chill.

- Wash and stem tomatoes. Cut tomatoes in wedges, petal fashion. Place on lettuce leaf, fill with chilled salad.

- Garnish with parsley or watercress.

- Serves 6.

PIONEER TOWN

The town of Cedaredge, just northeast of Delta, is in the process of completing a Pioneer Town, with restored buildings from its early beginnings. Included are a working blacksmith shop, Indian museum, ranch buildings and silos. A chapel and early fruit packing facility are also in the plans for this town with an eye for future tourism.

Earth Dance Pasta Salad

16 cups water

1 tsp salt

1 tsp vegetable oil

4 cups uncooked pasta

2 stalks broccoli, chopped

8 green onions, chopped

2 large Chem-Gro Tomatoes, chopped

1 large Chem-Gro Cucumber, peeled and chopped

6 stalks celery, chopped

1 cup green olives

12 marinated artichoke hearts, chopped

15-20 sticks Earth Dance Vegetarian Jerki

Dressing:

½ cup vinegar

¼ cup water

1¼ cups vegetable oil

¾ cup tamari or soy sauce

1 tsp garlic powder

½ tsp Colorado Spice Co. Cumin

2 tbsp chives

- Bring water, salt and oil to boil.
- Add pasta and cook until tender, 10 minutes.
- Drain, rinse and allow to cool.
- In very large bowl, combine vegetables, jerki and cooled pasta; mix well.
- Combine all dressing ingredients in covered container and shake well.
- Pour over salad and mix well.
- Makes 20 cups.

DELTA'S CONFLUENCE PARK

Visitors to Delta, Colorado, are greeted with murals depicting the area's industries, scenery and heritage. The colorful murals, painted by local artists, adorn the once bland buildings along the town's main street. Here, visitors will also find many opportunities for recreation and leisure activities. A decade of economic recession inspired some local residents to develop projects to interest vacationers and other visitors to their pristine area.

The new Delta Confluence Park, at the confluence of the Gunnison and Uncompahgre Rivers is in the midst of development. The park includes a walking trail and an outdoor amphitheatre in a spectacular setting. When complete, it will also encompass a fishing lake, a wildlife refuge area, an ice skating rink, a working replica of Fort Uncompahgre and family recreation facilities.

During the summer months, a pageant depicting the area's colorful history—entitled "Thunder Mountain Lives Tonight!"—is presented. The pageant portrays Ute culture and history, acted by actual Ute tribesmen from Ignacio.

Apple Chicken Salad

2 cups diced chicken, cooked or canned
1 cup sliced celery
½ cup sliced, pitted black olives
3 cups diced Colorado Apples
½ cup mayonnaise
¼ cup Meadow Gold Sour Cream
½ tsp lemon juice
⅛ tsp curry (optional)
salad greens
Colorado Apple Slices to garnish

- Combine chicken, celery, olives and apples.
- Combine mayonnaise, sour cream, lemon juice and curry.
- Mix dressing with chicken and apple mixture. Toss to coat evenly.
- Serve on salad greens garnished with apple slices.
- Serves 4-6.

Rafting on the Arkansas River, Buena Vista

Photo by Jeff Andrew

WILDFLOWERS

One of the things that makes Colorado's spring and summer months so rewarding is the abundance of wildflowers splashed across the countryside. It's best to purchase a good guide to identify these flowers, but here are some tips on some of the things you are likely to find: Fairyslipper, Alplily, Wild Iris, Bistort, Bitterroot, Columbine (the state's official flower), Fremont's Geranium, Goldenrod, Kinnikinnick, Little Red Elephant, Monkey Flower, Mountain Parsley, Potentilla, Woodnymph and so many others. It's difficult to imagine anything more stunning than a view stretching for as far as the eye can see filled with these treasures.

Summer Ravioli Salad

1 pkg Frangi's Mini-Cheese Ravioli
1 pkg Frangi's Mini-Meat Ravioli
1 jar marinated artichoke hearts
1 (15 oz) can garbanzo beans, drained
1 (6 oz) can large pitted black olives
1 (5 oz) can small green stuffed olives
1 jar roasted red peppers in oil
1 cup diced Leprino Mozzarella Cheese
1 cup diced Bar-S Salami or Sliced Pepperoni
1 (12 oz) btl Little Chalet Dressing

- Cook ravioli according to pkg directions; drain, rinse with cold water and set aside.
- Combine remaining ingredients, except salad dressing.
- Add ravioli to mixture and toss with Italian dressing.
- Chill at least 4 hours before serving.
- Serves 8.

A DINOSAUR NEST

For years, paleontologists combed the canyon country around Delta searching for the remains of great dinosaurs. In Wells Gulch, however, they found remnants of the smallest fossils, eggshells, that have opened up new insight into the prehistoric world that was Delta County 140 million years ago. Tests have confirmed that the eggshells show avian (bird) or dinosaurian characteristics, and the gulch is recognized as the oldest known dinosaur nest in North America.

Smoked Trout Mousse

oil

½ cup cold water

2 tsp unflavored gelatin

¾ cup mayonnaise

½ lb Arctic Pacific Smoked Trout Filets, flaked

½ cup finely chopped Grant Farms Celery

½ cup finely chopped cucumber

1½ tbsp finely chopped Bellwether Farms Dillweed

1 tbsp lemon juice

½ tsp salt

pinch white pepper

lettuce leaves

lemon wedges to garnish

Cucumber-Mint Sauce:
1 cup Yoplait Original Yogurt

¼ tsp chopped Bellwether Farms Mint

½ cup mayonnaise

¼ cup finely chopped cucumber

⅛ tsp garlic salt

- Oil 3-4 cup mold; set aside.
- Pour water into saucepan.
- Dissolve gelatin into water over low heat. Let cool.
- Combine in bowl with mayonnaise; stir in next 7 ingredients.
- Pour mixture into oiled mold. Refrigerate 3 hours until set.
- Combine all sauce ingredients in blender.
- To serve, invert mold on lettuce leaves. Pour on sauce. Garnish with lemon wedges.
- Serves 6-8.

THE GREAT DIVIDE

The Continental Divide physically divides Colorado into two parts, an Eastern and a Western slope. The two sections are now connected by the Eisenhower Memorial Tunnel, but previously trappers, miners, immigrants and even the railroad had to go around the towering granite barrier of the Divide. The 8,940 foot long tunnel eliminates a climb of 992 feet.

Sauerkraut Pinto Bean Salad

3 cups Red Bird Brand Cooked Pinto Beans
2 eggs, hard boiled, chilled and chopped
2 medium Tateys Onions, finely chopped
1 tsp salt
1 cup chopped, drained sauerkraut
mayonnaise
lettuce leaves
tomato wedges to garnish

- Mix all ingredients, except tomato and lettuce, adding just enough mayonnaise to moisten.
- Chill and serve on lettuce leaves.
- Garnish with tomato wedges.
- Serves 6-8.

Calico Salad

1 (11 oz) pkg Mitie Mixes Calico Soup Mix
5 cups water
1 medium OGI Onion, chopped
1 Inch By Inch Green Bell Pepper, chopped

Dressing:
½ cup vegetable oil
½ cup vinegar
½ cup GW Granulated Sugar
¼ tsp pepper

- Soak soup mix overnight. Drain.
- Add water, bring to boil and cook 1½ hours or until tender. Drain.
- Stir in onion and green pepper.
- Combine dressing ingredients and pour over bean mixture.
- Chill before serving. Best if marinated overnight.
- Serves 4.

RICHTOFEN CASTLE

Another of Denver's historic mansions is located in the east Denver neighborhood of Montclair. Richtofen Castle is truly a castle. Its unusual Prussian architecture is hidden behind large trees and foliage that grow inside the castle grounds. It is located at the corner of East Twelfth Avenue and Olive Streets, just south of East Colfax Avenue. Denver expanded along its two main streets, Broadway running north and south, and Colfax, running east and west.

Baron Walter von Richtofen, a burly, flamboyant German developer who was the uncle of the famous World War I flying ace "Red Baron" Manfred von Richtofen, planned an exclusive suburb to be located on a piece of open prairie four miles east of Broadway. He built his Prussian castle as his showcase home for the project.

Extra Creamy Potato Salad

2 lbs Russet Burbank Potatoes, cooked and cut into cubes

1 cup Mountain High® Plain Yoghurt, divided

¼ cup mayonnaise

¾ tsp dried dillweed

2 tsp Mady's Olde Time Beer Mustard

½ tsp salt

½ tsp pepper

1 cup shredded Swiss cheese

1 medium red or green pepper, chopped

2 green onions with tops, thinly sliced

- Toss potato cubes with ¼ cup of the yoghurt; cool to room temperature.
- Combine remaining yoghurt, mayonnaise, dillweed, mustard, salt and pepper. Add to potatoes, tossing to coat evenly.
- Stir in remaining ingredients.
- Chill, covered, 2-3 hours to allow flavors to blend.
- Serves 6.

RICHTOFEN'S SUBURB

When Baron Walter von Richtofen started his development outside of Denver, the obsessed developer was too impatient to wait until the streetcar line could be extended to reach his property. So he operated an elegant horse-drawn tally-ho coach to carry potential lot buyers to the site. The coach would pick them up in front of the Tabor Opera House in Denver and carry them four miles across dusty flatland dotted by only a few farm houses, while Richtofen dashed ahead on his own steed. Few actually purchased property before the streetcar line got that far east, and the area did not really develop into a suburb until the automobile came into use in the 1920s. Until recent years, its centerpiece, Richtofen Castle, was open for tours and civic events, but today it is privately owned and not available for touring.

Oriental Salad

1 lb Life Force Foods Bean Sprouts

6 green onions, finely chopped

6 stalks celery, chopped

1 (4 oz) jar chopped pimento

½ lb Rakhra Mushrooms, sliced

1 tsp dillweed

2 tbsp minced parsley

1½ tbsp sesame seeds

1 lb boiled Keeton Fisheries Baby Shrimp (optional)

Dressing:

¼ cup rice vinegar

¼ cup soy sauce

¼ cup Graham's Golden Honey

½ cup peanut oil

2 tbsp sesame concentrate oil

salt and pepper

- Toss together salad ingredients.
- Mix all dressing ingredients together in blender and toss well with salad.
- Chill at least 1 hour.
- Serve as side salad or add shrimp for main course.
- Serves 4-6.

BLUE SPRUCE CAPITAL

Examples of the state tree, the Blue Spruce, can be seen while touring Colorado's mountain highways, and the small town of Evergreen, Colorado, calls itself the Blue Spruce Capital of the World. Depending upon elevation and water supply, the color may vary from silvery blue to blue-green, or grey-green. A cousin to the blue spruce, the Englemann spruce, is often mistaken for it. The Englemann, however, has foliage that is soft and pliable.

In higher ranges, where the two grow together, they occasionally form hybrids, which are difficult to distinguish from the pure varieties. The state tree is hardy, long-lived and susceptible to relatively few insect and diseases. These factors, and its beauty, explain its popularity as an ornamental.

Layered Salad

2 cups chopped spinach
2 cups Life Force Foods Spicy Sprouts
1 cup chopped celery
1 cup chopped Life Force Foods Green Bell Pepper
1 cup peanuts
1 cup chopped green onions
1 cup frozen peas, thawed
1½ cups mayonnaise
1½ tbsp sugar
grated Cheddar cheese
crisply cooked Bar-S Bacon, crumbled
1 egg, hard boiled and chopped

- In order given, layer first 7 ingredients in salad bowl.
- Spread top with mayonnaise.
- Sprinkle sugar on top of mayonnaise.
- Sprinkle grated cheese on top to cover.
- Refrigerate 5 hours.
- When ready to serve, garnish with bacon and egg.
- Serves 6-8.

Zippy Cole Slaw

1-2 tbsp Joy's Chili Pepper Jelly, Hot or Mild

½ cup Rosalie's Cole Slaw Dressing

4 cups cole slaw

- Blend pepper jelly and dressing well.
- Stir into cole slaw.
- Serves 4.

Cranberry Walnut Salad

¾ cup chopped Naturally Nuts Walnuts

1 cup uncooked, coarsley chopped cranberries

¼ cup GW Granulated Sugar

2 (3 oz) pkgs lemon gelatin

1¾ cups boiling water

3 tbsp lemon juice

¼ tsp salt

1 (8.25 oz) can pineapple chunks

1 (10 oz) btl 7Up

1 (8 oz) pkg cream cheese, softened

salad greens

- Toast nuts at 300 degrees 10 minutes; set aside.
- Mix cranberries with sugar. Let stand while preparing salad.
- Dissolve gelatin in boiling water.
- Stir in lemon juice and salt.
- Drain syrup from pineapple into gelatin mixture. Cool thoroughly.
- Stir in 7Up. Cool until thickened.
- Set aside 1½ cups of gelatin mixture for cheese layer.
- Stir cranberries, pineapple and half the walnuts into remaining clear gelatin.
- Spoon into 6 cup mold; chill.
- Meanwhile, blend cream cheese into reserved gelatin.
- Stir in walnuts.
- When fruit layer is almost set, carefully spoon creamy mixture on top.
- Chill several hours or overnight until firm.
- Unmold onto salad greens to serve.
- Serves 8.

DESERT IN COLORADO?

Thinking of Colorado does not conjure up visions of expansive tracts of desert land. Yet, that is just what one can expect at the Great Sand Dunes National Monument in the San Luis Valley of southern Colorado. Nestled next to the fabulous Sangre de Cristo Mountains, it is one of the state's most unusual geologic features. The monument encompasses 150 square miles that includes the tallest sand dunes in all of North America, some rising to over 700 feet. According to geological reports, the dunes are the result of massive ancient glaciers, which, over 10,000 years ago, covered the high peaks that form the valley. When the glaciers receded, gravel, sand and silt was carried by water to the valley floor and deposited along the river banks. Once picked up by the winds which flow across the valley, tiny grains of sand are carried eastward toward the Sangre de Cristo mountains.

Cranberry Sour Cream Mold

Mold:

1 (6 oz) pkg raspberry flavored gelatin

1½ cups boiling water

2 (10 oz) pkgs frozen cranberry-orange relish

Dressing:

¼ cup Marquest Orange Juice

1 tbsp grated orange peel

½ tsp Colorado Spice Co. Vanilla

1 cup Meadow Gold Sour Cream

- Dissolve gelatin in boiling water.
- Break up frozen cranberry relish with fork; add to gelatin mixture and stir until cranberry relish is thoroughly thawed and combined with gelatin.
- Pour into 6 cup mold; chill until set, preferably overnight.
- For dressing, stir orange juice, peel and vanilla gently into sour cream.
- Serve with cranberry mold.
- Serves 12.

THE DUNES

When southwesterly valley winds reach the high peaks of the Sangre de Cristo Mountains they are trapped. Upon losing speed, they drop sand and silt at the base of the mountains. Over time the small sand deposits built into huge dunes, thus forming the Great Sand Dunes National Monument in the San Luis Valley. Even today, the dunes are constantly changing. Visiting the dunes, one can actually observe the sand's movement.

Proclaimed a national monument in 1932, the awesome sights and interesting history surrounding the life forms that have lived there, is well worth the trip.

Pico de Gallo Salad

2 cups Rakhra Mushrooms, chopped
2 large tomatoes, chopped
½ cup sliced green onions
1 (14 oz) jar Championship Recipe Poultry Marinade
8 oz fresh spinach, cleaned and trimmed

- Combine mushrooms, tomatoes and onions.
- Shake marinade well; pour half of jar over mushroom mixture.
- Cover and chill 3-24 hours, stirring occasionally.
- Before serving, drain mixture well.
- In bowl, combine with fresh spinach, torn into pieces.
- Serves 4-6.

Sunflower Guacamole

1 ripe avocado, mashed
2 Thomas Produce Tomatoes, diced
1 red bell pepper, diced
¼ cup grated Thomas Produce Onion
½-1 cup chopped Campion Greenhouse Sunflower Sprouts
1 lemon, juiced
⅛ tsp garlic salt

- Mix avocado, tomatoes, bell pepper, onion and sprouts together.
- Add lemon juice and garlic salt.
- Mix well.
- Serves 4.

APPLE COUNTRY

Just south of Grand Junction, Colorado, lies Delta County, the heart of the state's largest fruit crop—apples. Over three-fourths of the state's apples are grown here, near the North Fork of the Gunnison River. Visitors traveling through the small communities of Delta, Hotchkiss, Paonia and Cedaredge, at the southern base of Grand Mesa, are readily aware of the importance of the fruit industry. Orchards, packing facilities and fruit-for-sale stands are common sights. From mid-September through October, the area bustles.

Spinach Apple Toss

2 bunches spinach, washed
2 apples, cored and diced
4 slices Bar-S Bacon, cooked crisp, crumbled
¼ cup Life Force Foods Sprouts
1 small avocado, peeled and diced (optional)

Dressing:
½ cup mayonnaise
¼ cup Mountain High® Plain Yoghurt
2 tsp granulated sugar or honey
1 tbsp red wine vinegar

- Tear spinach into bite-size pieces.
- Add remaining salad ingredients; toss.
- Mix dressing ingredients together and toss with salad.
- Serve immediately.
- Serves 4-6.

SWEET FRUITS

Just to the south of Delta County is Montrose County. Together they enjoy one of the country's most favorable fruit and vegetable growing environments. Clean air, long days of sunshine, cool nights and ample high quality water. They combine to provide a growing climate that produces crisp vegetables and sweet fruit—the envy of growers throughout the world. Besides apples, the area produces peaches, pears, cherries, raspberries, lettuce, onions, sweet corn and broccoli.

The bountiful area, and that continuing south to Gunnison, is home to some of the most dramatic terrain on the continent. Steep pitched spires contrast with deep plunging canyons. Shadowed forests open to lush valleys. In the fall, while farmers are hard at work bringing in the crops before the first early freeze, the area is host to sportsmen from throughout the world. The abundant wildlife and water, which provided subsistence for the area's earlier residents, Ute Indian tribes, now attracts thousands of hunters, and water sports enthusiasts.

Beer Curried Fruit

1 (1 lb 14 oz) can pear halves
1 (1 lb 14 oz) can peach slices
2 (11 oz) cans mandarin oranges
1 tbsp Colorado Spice Co. Curry Powder
2 tbsp lemon juice
1 cup Budweiser® Beer
grated rind of 1 orange
1 banana, sliced
fresh strawberries, halved

- Drain canned fruits and reserve combined syrup.
- Place fruits in large saucepan. Cover fruit with reserved syrup.
- Blend curry powder with lemon juice; add to fruit.
- Add beer and orange rind. Stir gently.
- Simmer mixture 5 minutes, or until heated thoroughly.
- Fold in fresh fruits.
- Serve warm or chilled.
- Serves 8.

SAUCES

Bull Riding in Monte Vista

Photo by Art Bilsten

REAL HIGH COUNTRY

Colorado has fifty-three mountain peaks stretching above 14,000 feet and 1,142 peaks over 10,000 feet high. The 14,264-foot pinnacle of Mount Evans may be reached by driving up the highest mountain road in America.

Rocky Mountain National Park is high, wide and breathtaking in its vast spaciousness. In it you will find 410 square miles of forested, towering mountain land clustered with eighty-four peaks of jagged majesty looming skyward over 11,000 feet. At the top is 14,256-foot Longs Peak. Rocky Mountain National Park is open all year; every season offers different dimensions of enjoyment.

Caribbean Creole Curry Sauce

4 tbsp chopped green pepper
4 tbsp chopped onion
4 tbsp chopped celery
1 small clove garlic, chopped
1 (7 oz) can unsweetened coconut milk
1½ cups half and half
5 tbsp Lucile's Caribbean Creole Curry Seasoning
salt

- Blend vegetables, garlic and coconut milk in food processor.
- Transfer to medium pot.
- Add cream and seasoning to vegetables; boil until vegetables are cooked and sauce is thick.
- Add salt to taste.
- Makes 3½ cups.

Mustard Grill Sauce for Meat or Chicken

4 tbsp More Than Mustard Country Style, Original Recipe or Raspberry Flavor Mustard
2 tbsp tamari
1 tbsp fresh lemon juice

- Combine all ingredients.
- Brush mixture on chicken or beef before grilling.
- Makes ¼ cup.

RED ROCKS PARK

Travel west of Denver to the small community of Morrison and you'll find an amazing geological sight—Red Rocks Park. The red sandstone formations, thrust dramatically upward during formation of the Rockies, are stunning. In the middle of this wonder is a natural outdoor amphitheatre. Seat yourself there and watch the colors emerge through the various stages of light. You'll be mesmerized by the beauty of the color changes in the rocks. Because the amphitheatre faces east, daybreak is a most beautiful time to spend there.

Sauce for Roast Pork

⅔ cup brewed strong Boyer's Coffee
⅓ cup Robinson Unsalted Butter
2 tsp F & J Worcestershire Sauce
1½ tsp dry mustard
1 tbsp lemon juice
1 tsp sugar
F & J Piqueosot Sauce to taste

- Combine all ingredients in saucepan. Heat gently until butter melts.
- Brush over pork during roasting.
- Serve remaining sauce in sauceboat.
- Makes 1¼ cups.

Spaghetti Sauce

1 lb ground beef
1 cup diced celery
1 small onion, diced
½ bell pepper, diced
1 (6 oz) can Cream of the Valley Tomato Paste
1½ cups water
1 tsp Italian seasoning
1 tsp Dixon & Sons Q-Mix
Dixon Steak Sauce

- In skillet, sauté ground beef, celery, onion and bell pepper.
- Add tomato paste, water and seasonings.
- Stir in steak sauce to taste.
- Simmer 30 minutes-1 hour, stirring occasionally.
- Makes 4 cups.

SLOW TRAIN TO SILVERTON

If you're interested in trains, then Durango-Silverton is the place to go in Colorado. Located in the Southwest part of the state these towns are served by a narrow-gauge railroad that's a focus of tourist interest.

The Denver and Rio Grande Railroad founded Durango in 1880. Shortly thereafter the narrow-gauge rails were extended north through Animas Canyon with the first train arriving in Silverton in 1882. During the summer months, taking the train from Durango to Silverton and back is an exciting adventure. The round trip is approximately eight hours. Smoke billows onto everyone and everything during the trip, and at an average speed of sixteen miles per hour it is a long ride. But the rugged terrain along the Los Animas River is famous for its natural beauty and is ample compensation

Four wheeling or hiking are two of the most attractive pursuits upon arrival in the area, as San Juan County was once the home of many mining towns and camps. Driving into the area you will pass some of the most spectacular scenery anywhere in Colorado.

Barbecue Sauce

2 cups ketchup
½ cup F & J Steak Sauce
2 tbsp vinegar
½ cup brown sugar
or
⅓ cup molasses
⅓ cup F & J Worcestershire Sauce
⅓ cup Cream of the Valley Tomato Paste
⅓ tsp F & J Chili Powder
1 clove

- Place all ingredients in medium saucepan and cook over low heat 30 minutes, stirring occasionally to prevent sticking.
- Especially good with oven-cooked spare ribs.
- Makes 3½ cups.

ANTIQUING

Antique Row in Denver has numerous stores that exhibit the history of Colorado through the variety of items available there. Rusted barbed wire, dressers, lamps and more are all on display, and for sale, in buildings which are originals themselves, dating back to the late 1800s.

Colorado Salsa

1 (28 oz) can whole, peeled Diven Tomatoes

1 clove garlic, chopped

1 onion, chopped

chopped green chilies and jalapeno peppers

1 tbsp vinegar

chopped cilantro or oregano to taste

salt to taste

- Stir all ingredients together adding green chilies and jalapeno peppers to taste.
- Serve freshly made and cold as side dish with Mexican food, or as dip for tortilla chips.
- Makes 3½ cups.

Roasted Pecan Salad Dressing

4 cups pecans

½ cup butter

2 cups vegetable oil

4 lemons, juiced

3 tbsp Worcestershire sauce

1 tsp Lucile's Famous Creole Seasoning-Original

½ tsp hot pepper sauce

1 tsp minced garlic

1 tsp salt

1 cup chopped green onions

- Roast pecans in 400 degree oven 10 minutes.
- In blender, add butter to roasted pecans.
- Slowly add oil until blended.
- Add remaining ingredients.
- Makes 3 cups.

SUNNY DENVER

Weather in Colorado is a real fooler to most. It is estimated that Denver has over 315 days of sunshine each year. Nights are cool and humidity is low. Western slopes of the Rockies get the most moisture, and temperatures in mountain valleys can dip to sixty degrees below zero in the winter. However, chinook winds often blow down the eastern slopes during the winters and can raise temperatures markedly within a few hours.

Buttermilk/Bleu Cheese Dressing

1 cup Meadow Gold Old Style Buttermilk
2 cups mayonnaise
¼ onion, chopped
1 tbsp F & J Worcestershire Sauce
¼ tsp All American Seasonings Garlic Powder
1 cup crumbled bleu cheese, divided

- Put first 5 ingredients and half the cheese in blender.
- Cover, and blend on high until smooth.
- Add remaining cheese in large chunks, cover and blend on high 6 seconds, or until coarsely chopped.
- Makes 1 qt.

Mocha Sundae Sauce

1 cup Rocky Mountain Butter, softened
2 cups Holly Powdered Sugar
2 tbsp cocoa
2 tbsp instant coffee
⅛ tsp salt
2 eggs
2 tsp vanilla
ice cream or pound cake

- Beat butter, sugar, cocoa, coffee and salt until smooth and creamy.
- Add eggs; blend well.
- Place in saucepan; heat, stirring constantly, until sauce is thickened and fluffy.
- Blend in vanilla.
- Serve warm over ice cream or pound cake.
- Makes 2¼ cups.

IT'S A FACT

Yes, Greeley, Colorado was established by famous *New York Tribune* editor Horace Greeley. It is an agricultural marketing center north and east of Denver.

Savory Yoghurt Dressing

1 cup Mountain High® Plain Yoghurt
¼ cup water
½ tsp All American Seasonings Garlic Powder
½ tsp All American Seasonings Paprika
¼ tsp salt
⅛ tsp hot pepper sauce

- In small bowl, combine ingredients.
- Cover; chill several hours to blend flavors.
- Makes 1¼ cups.

Peach Spread

1 (8 oz) pkg cream cheese, softened
½ cup GW Powdered Sugar, sifted
⅛ tsp almond extract
1 cup finely diced Colorado Peaches
crackers or peach bread slices

- Beat cream cheese until smooth and fluffy.
- Add sugar; mix well.
- Add almond flavoring and peaches; mix gently.
- Spread on crackers or peach bread slices.
- Makes 1½ cups.

Creamy Honey Vanilla Dressing for Fruit

1½ cups Mountain High® Honey Vanilla Yoghurt
2 tbsp orange juice
½ tsp grated orange rind

- In small bowl, combine ingredients.
- Cover; chill several hours to blend flavors.
- Refrigerate leftovers.
- Makes 1½ cups.

VEGETABLES

Miracle Rock in Glade Park

Photo by Ron Ruhoff

LEGEND OF THE GRAND MESA

The Indians had their own legend for the many lakes that were clustered upon the Grand Mesa, east of Grand Junction. One day, it was said, a great thunderbird that lived along the rim of the mesa flew away with an Indian child. The child's father disguised himself in the bark of a tree and slowly crept up to the base of the mesa, where a large serpent devoured them both. Enraged thunderbirds snared the serpent and carried him high above the mountain peaks, ripping him to pieces. When the pieces plunged to the earth, they tore deep pits into the ground. So great was the rage of the thunderbirds that the land shook with thunder. Torrents of rain filled the pits, and they formed the great lakes of Grand Mesa.

Stuffed Potatoes with Cheese and Chilies

4 large San Luis Valley Baking Potatoes
salt and pepper
4 tbsp chopped black olives
½ cup canned, diced green chilies
4-6 tbsp Golden Peaks Heavy Cream
½ cup grated sharp Cheddar cheese
grated Cheddar cheese to top
*sour cream and whole black olives
to garnish*

- Bake potatoes until done.
- Cool; cut off tops and scrape out pulp, being careful not to tear shells. Reserve pulp.
- Salt and pepper shells; set aside.
- Mash pulp; stir in olives, chilies and enough cream to give mixture desired consistency.
- Season to taste with salt and pepper; stir in cheese.
- Divide potato mixture equally among shells, mounding filling slightly.
- Sprinkle with more cheese, if desired, and bake again at 400 degrees until potatoes are hot and cheese is bubbly.
- Top each potato with spoonful of sour cream and an olive.
- Serves 4.

THE AWE OF ESTES PARK

The quaint little resort city of Estes Park nestled on the edge of Rocky Mountain National Park, surrounded by the high country walls of America's most breathtaking mountain range. Milton Estes wrote of his 1859 discovery of the landscape:

"We stood on the mountain looking down at the headwaters of Little Thompson Creek, where the park spread out before us. No words can describe our surprise, wonder, and joy at beholding such an unexpected sight."

Rufus B. Sage explored the land, and he wrote: "It seemed, indeed, like a concentration of beautiful lateral valleys, intersected by meandering watercourses, ridged by lofty ledges of precipitous rock, and hemmed in upon the west by vast piles of mountains, climbing beyond the clouds. . . ."

Country Style Pinto Beans

2 cups dry Red Bird Brand Pinto Beans
4-6 cups water
4 slices Banes Bacon, diced
1 tsp salt
1 tsp savory salt
¼ cup minced onion
6 tbsp Cream of the Valley Tomato Paste
2 tbsp butter or bacon grease
prepared corn bread

- Soak beans overnight; drain.
- Put in pressure cooker; cover with warm water, 2" above beans.
- Add remaining ingredients, except corn bread; stir well.
- Cook 45 minutes at 10 lbs pressure.
- Remove lid; cook, uncovered, until juice is thick.
- Serve with corn bread.
- Serves 6-8.

Mesa Verde

Photo by Lou Poulter

PORTRAIT OF A PROSPECTOR

The great Rocky Mountains beckoned to those who sought to find wealth by taking gold from its hiding places. One swore that all it took to get rich was "pluck, perseverance, and a pick, supplemented by pork and provender."

Estes Park resident, Joe Mills, described those old prospectors this way: "They are all picturesque characters, living in a world of golden dreams, oblivious to everything but the hole they are digging, the gold they are sure to find."

Mexicali Potato Pie

1½ lbs San Luis Valley White Potatoes, scrubbed

1 onion, minced

¼ tsp Colorado Spice Co. Red Pepper Flakes

5 tbsp olive oil

2 large eggs, lightly beaten

¼ lb Monterey Jack cheese, grated

1 (4 oz) can chopped green chilies

½ cup chopped black olives

1 tbsp fresh lemon juice, or to taste

salt and pepper

6 tbsp dry bread crumbs

- Boil potatoes until tender. Drain, cool and peel.
- Force potatoes through ricer or food mill into large bowl.
- In small skillet, cook onion with red pepper in 2 tbsp of the oil until onion is soft.
- Add to potatoes along with eggs, cheese, chilies, olives, lemon juice, and salt and pepper to taste; combine well.
- Coat bottom and sides of 9″ pie pan with 1 tbsp of oil and coat pan with 3 tbsp bread crumbs.
- Spread potato mixture in pan, sprinkle with remaining crumbs and drizzle remaining 2 tbsp oil over top.
- Bake in 350 degree oven 1 hour.
- Cool on rack 5 minutes; cut into wedges.
- Serve warm.
- Serves 4-6.

D&RG VERSUS THE SANTA FE

Warfare existed between the Denver and Rio Grande Railroad and the Santa Fe for routes into Colorado, especially to the rich gold and silver fields. However, in a compromise reached after much legal wrangling, the D&RG was given expansion rights into Colorado and the railroad plunged into the effort, moving into Leadville and Durango. Unfortunately for General William Jackson Palmer, head of the D&RG, the story has a sad outcome. Legal battles with the Santa Fe had stretched the D&RG resources and eventually Palmer was forced to turn the railroad over to Eastern interests headed by Jay Gould. In the long run though, that action may also have benefited Colorado, as the General turned his energies to developing Colorado Springs into "the most attractive place for residence in the entire West."

Cusat

2 tbsp vegetable oil

2 large San Luis Valley Potatoes, peeled and cut into large pieces

1 A-V Onion, chopped

½ cup water

2 zucchini squash, sliced

1 Life Force Green Bell Pepper, cut into small pieces

2-3 Life Force Tomatoes, chopped

salt, pepper and garlic powder

- Heat oil in large skillet.
- Brown potatoes and onion; add water and simmer 10 minutes.
- Add zucchini, bell pepper and tomatoes; simmer until done, 30-40 minutes.
- While simmering, add salt, pepper and garlic powder to taste.
- Serves 4-6.

TRADING AT FORT VASQUEZ

A pair of rugged mountain men, taking advantage of the rugged wilderness around them, fashioned Fort Vasquez in the 1830s, opening its doors to Indian trade along the South Platte River. Louis Vasquez and Andrew Sublette developed quite a business, trading black silk handkerchiefs, ivory combs, Hudson Bay blankets and brass kettles for valuable Indian buffalo robes.

Although abandoned in 1842, the fort, surrounded by twelve foot walls, has been reconstructed at Platteville.

Chef Mickey's Famous Red Beans

3 cups small red beans
1 large green pepper, chopped
3 stalks celery, chopped
1 small onion, chopped
2 tbsp vegetable oil
½ gal water
1 bay leaf
1 tbsp Worcestershire sauce
1 tsp hot pepper sauce
2 smoked ham hocks
2½ tbsp Lucile's Famous Creole Seasoning

- Soak beans overnight, covered with water 2″ above beans.
- The next day, before cooking, drain beans and set aside.
- In large pot, sauté green pepper, celery and onion in oil.
- Add beans, water, bay leaf, Worcestershire sauce, pepper sauce, ham hocks and Creole seasoning; bring to boil over high heat.
- Lower heat and simmer, uncovered, 3-4 hours, or until beans are tender.
- Add water as needed, depending on evaporation.
- Discard bay leaf and ham hock bones. Break up any large pieces of meat remaining.
- Serves 6-8.

HOME OF THE ANCIENT ONES

Those who came to carve their homes into the cliffs of Mesa Verde, near Cortez, were called "Anasazi," the ancient ones. They were nomads who found refuge in the mountains around 400 to 1300 A.D. No one really knows who they were. No one really knows their origin. They clustered into tribes upon a strange land that would forever become their home. All they left behind were their cliff dwellings, their ruins.

Anasazi Beans® and Ham Hocks

2 cups dry Anasazi Beans®, washed
6 cups water
2 ham hocks
1 large Tateys Onion, quartered
2 cloves garlic, pressed
salt and pepper
El Grande Tortillas

- Cook beans in water, at gentle boil, until almost done.
- Keep covered with water while cooking.
- Add ham hocks, onion, garlic, and salt and pepper to taste.
- Cook until done.
- Serve with tortillas.
- Serves 6-8.

Fried Beans Deluxe

4 cups cooked Red Bird Brand Pinto Beans
vegetable oil
6 La Tolteca Corn Tortillas
1 cup grated Cheddar cheese

- Place 1 cup beans at a time, reserving ¼ cup whole beans, in hot pan with small amount of oil.
- Mash with potato masher; fry lightly.
- Add ¼ cup whole beans.
- In another pan, crumble tortillas; fry in hot oil until crisp.
- Place beans in casserole; top with crisp tortilla pieces.
- Sprinkle with cheese; bake at 325 degrees until cheese is melted.
- Serves 6-8.

MESA VERDE'S FIRST "TOWNHOUSES"

Carved into the cliffs of Mesa Verde National Park are the dwellings of the Indians that once inhabited this part of the Rockies. A step into what some term America's first townhouses is a step into the long-ago of this country's history and a fascinating insight into a culture still preserved through the skills of ancient architecture.

Mexicali Jumping Mushrooms

1 cup shredded sharp Cheddar cheese
¼ cup Meadow Gold Sour Cream
3 tbsp sliced green onions
2½ tbsp chopped cilantro
3 tbsp canned diced green chilies
¼ cup Meadow Gold Butter
1 clove garlic, minced
18, 2" Rakhra Mushroom Caps
1¼ cups grated Parmesan cheese

- In mixing bowl, toss Cheddar cheese, sour cream, onions, cilantro and chilies to mix evenly; set aside.
- In small saucepan, combine butter and garlic; warm over low heat to melt butter.
- Brush mushroom caps with garlic butter.
- Fill each cap with about 1 tbsp cheese mixture.
- Sprinkle generously with Parmesan cheese.
- Broil until bubbly and golden, about 3 minutes.
- Serves 6-8.

Refried Anasazi Beans®

6 cups water
2 cups dried Anasazi Beans®
1 tsp chili powder
¼ cup finely chopped onion
¼ cup finely chopped green pepper
1 clove garlic, crushed
6 slices Bar-S Bacon, chopped
2 tbsp Rocky Mountain Butter

- Add water, beans and chili powder in large pan; cook, at gentle boil, 1½ hours, or until tender.
- Drain beans, saving liquid.
- Sauté onion, green pepper, garlic and bacon in butter.
- Mash beans together with sautéed mixture, adding liquid, a little at a time, until bean mixture is smooth.
- Serves 6-8.

BOULDER'S HENDERSON MUSEUM

It is a rainy Saturday afternoon and your children are bored and asking: "How deep is the Ocean? How did the mountains get here?" It's time to get into the car and drive to Boulder for a visit to the Henderson Museum. The permanent exhibits are tied to the themes of man, earth and life. Carvings and costumes, such as a Samurai Warrior's outfit, also provide interesting answers to difficult questions. Dinosaurs are extensively featured as well. Of course the interesting exhibits probably will spark further questions, so plan to return many more times for all the answers.

Eggplant Parmesan

1 medium eggplant
olive oil
1 (15 oz) ctn Chapin's Supreme Pasta Sauce
8 oz mozzarella cheese, sliced
grated Parmesan cheese

- Peel and slice eggplant into ½″ crosswise slices; brown slices in small amount of olive oil in non-stick pan.
- Place browned slices in baking pan, cover with pasta sauce and mozzarella slices.
- Sprinkle with Parmesan cheese and bake at 350 degrees 20 minutes.
- Serves 4.

Crisp Golden Mushrooms

⅓ cup corn flake crumbs
½ tsp Italian seasoning
¼ tsp salt
dash ground red pepper
½ lb Rakhra Mushrooms, washed and trimmed
¼ cup Graves Dairy Light Cream

- Preheat oven to 350 degrees.
- Place corn flake crumbs, seasoning, salt and red pepper into small paper or plastic bag; shake well.
- Dip mushrooms into cream; shake with seasoned cornflakes.
- Place mushrooms on cookie sheet and bake 15 minutes.
- Serves 8-10.

Brazilian Black Beans

Beans:

1 (11 oz) pkg Mitie Mixes Black Beans

8 cups water

¼ lb sliced pork hock

¼ lb chuck steak

1 lb Old West Italian Sausage

¼ lb salt pork

1 clove garlic, minced

¼ cup chopped onion

½ cup chopped tomato

2 tsp vegetable oil

rice

hot sauce

sliced oranges to garnish

Rice:

1 clove garlic, minced

¼ cup chopped onion

1 tomato, chopped

2 tsp vegetable oil

2 cups water

1 cup rice

Hot Sauce:

½ cup finely chopped onion

2 cups boiling water

3 tbsp vegetable oil

3 tbsp wine vinegar

3 tbsp cayenne pepper sauce

- Combine beans, water, pork hock, chuck steak, Italian sausage and salt pork; cook 1½ hours.
- Sauté garlic, onion and tomato in oil.
- Add to bean mixture.
- Cook 1 hour more, or until beans are tender and sauce is thick.
- To prepare rice, brown garlic, onion and tomato in oil; add water and rice.
- Simmer, covered, 15 minutes.
- For hot sauce, place onion in strainer.
- Pour boiling water over onion.
- Combine onion with oil, wine vinegar and cayenne pepper sauce.
- Serve beans over rice with hot sauce.
- Serves 8-10.

STEAMBOAT SPRINGS

At the height of the silver boom, rumors of sudden wealth had little affect on residents of Steamboat Springs, a tiny cattle town in the northwestern Yampa Valley. Its settlers were largely concerned with cattle ranching.

The face of the little town began to change in 1913, when the late Carl Howelsen brought the excitement of skiing from his homeland of Scandinavia. Steamboat Springs became the first town in North America to celebrate a Winter Carnival. Today, it is one of the Rocky Mountain's finest year-round resorts, and has enjoyed the title of "Ski Town, U.S.A." It has been the training ground for numerous U.S. Olympic skiers, and skiing is even taught as part of the local educational curriculum.

In the surrounding forests reside the largest elk herd in the nation, along with native deer. Lakes and streams provide plenty of sailboating, waterskiing and fishing in this rustic area where man and nature co-exist.

Microwaved Baked Apples

4 medium Colorado Baking Apples
3 tbsp packed brown sugar
1 tbsp Rocky Mountain Butter, softened
½ tsp cinnamon

- Core apples, being careful not to cut through completely. Peel ⅓ of the apple.
- Blend brown sugar, butter and cinnamon.
- Fill center of each apple.
- Arrange in 9″ round glass dish, forming ring.
- Cover with vented plastic wrap and microwave on HIGH 6-7 minutes.
- Let stand, covered, 5 minutes.
- Test for doneness; if necessary, microwave an additional 1-2 minutes.
- Serves 4.

DENVER'S TATTERED COVER

On a rainy Saturday afternoon, it seems you will find most Denverites packed onto the three floors of one of the United States', and maybe even the world's, most fascinating bookstores, The Tattered Cover. Whether you are looking for foreign periodicals, or a how-to text on Kung Fu, or the best of out-of-state newspapers, the store has it all. You might travel the world and find stores with more volumes on single subjects, or with more rare books, or with more obscure books, but it will be hard to beat the total number of books on so many different subjects. Staff members are exceptionally skilled on knowing where a specific book will be located. There is even a map of the store to help you find your way through. And most weeks, there is at least one author in the store autographing. Whether its raining or not, The Tattered Cover is a must stop on a Denver itinerary.

Apple Stuffing

4 medium Colorado Apples, peeled, cored and sliced

2 tbsp sugar (optional)

½ cup butter

2½-3 cups Skyland Apple Juice

2 (6 oz) pkgs chicken flavor stuffing mix

- Sprinkle apple slices with sugar; sauté in butter in large skillet until barely tender.
- Add apple juice (for more moist stuffing, use 3 cups apple juice) and contents of stuffing/seasoning packets; bring to boil.
- Pour into 2 qt casserole.
- Stir in stuffing crumbs, mixing lightly.
- Bake, uncovered, at 350 degrees 15 minutes.
- Serves 16.

TELLURIDE'S NEW GOLD

"To hell you ride," was the gold miner's pet name for Telluride, whose mines produced over $300 million. Country and western singer Willie Nelson called it the most beautiful spot he had ever seen. Jazz musician Dizzy Gillespie trumpeted that "If this isn't paradise, then heaven can wait."

The town's name came from the crystalline element, tellurium, found in a compound with gold and silver. The spectacular San Juan Mountains surround Telluride, located in southwestern Colorado. Butch Cassidy robbed his first bank in the town. Telluride was "rediscovered" and refurbished in the 1960s. Besides being one of the finest ski areas in the world, the town consists of one main street just two blocks from the back country. Music festivals draw large crowds to the area each summer.

Scalloped Corn

¼ cup chopped A-V Onion
2 tbsp margarine
1 (17 oz) can cream-style corn
2 eggs, slightly beaten
18 Ritz Crackers, crushed
½ cup shredded Cheddar cheese

- Preheat oven to 375 degrees.
- Sauté onion and margarine together until onion is tender.
- In medium bowl, combine onion, corn, eggs, cracker crumbs and cheese.
- Stir until well blended.
- Pour into greased 1 qt casserole.
- Bake 35-40 minutes, or until lightly browned and set.
- Serves 4-6.

GEM OF THE ROCKIES

Ouray, known as the "Gem of the Rockies," sometimes seems to be trapped by the high country, walled in by towering cliffs.

The town is only a quarter of a mile wide and a half mile long, and it rests in the heart of the Uncompahgre National Forest, secluded at an elevation of 7,800 feet in the San Juan Mountains. In the beginning, it owed its existence to the discovery of silver. But, during the Silver Panic of 1893, the value of the ore abruptly fell, and Ouray found itself perched on the threshold of disaster.

But Ouray did not wither away. Silver may have been worthless, but Ouray also had gold in its hills. From 1896 to 1910, the Camp Bird Mine alone produced $26 million.

Artichokes Alla Romagna

1 (16 oz) can unmarinated artichoke hearts

1 tbsp Rocky Mountain Butter

1 (12 oz) ctn Chapin's Supreme Alfredo Sauce

cooked linguine or penne

slivered almonds, toasted

- Drain artichokes and slice thin.
- Sauté in butter 1 minute.
- Stir in alfredo sauce; heat until bubbly.
- Serve on linguine or penne.
- Sprinkle with slivered almonds before serving.
- Serves 4.

Apple Raisin Rice Pilaf

1 small onion, chopped

1 cup rice

2 tbsp butter

2 cups Skyland Apple Juice

1 Colorado Apple, cored and sliced

½ cup Leroux Creek Raisins

1 tsp cinnamon

- Sauté onion and rice in butter until golden brown.
- Add remaining ingredients.
- Over low heat simmer, covered, 15 minutes, or until liquid is absorbed.
- Serves 4.

PASTA

San Juan Mountains

Photo by Jeff Andrew

VOLCANIC FOSSILS

The ancient calligraphy of life has been inscribed in the rocks of the Florissant Fossil Beds National Monument, not far from Ute Pass and the town of Florissant.

The fossils themselves are preserved in the dried remnants of a lake that existed 38 million years ago, a lake formed when flows of lava and mud spread across the valley. For almost 500,000 years, intermittent explosions showered millions of tons of dust and pumice into the air, and it trapped a large variety of plants and animals in layers of fine-grained ash.

The fossils in the lakebed were discovered in 1874. And since then, scientists from around the world have removed more than 80,000 specimens from the shale. Fossils of fishes, birds, small mammals, plants, and more than a thousand species of insects have been identified in the rare valley.

Salmon Tetrazzini

1 (8 oz) pkg noodles with chicken broth and almonds dinner

1 tbsp Rocky Mountain Butter

⅓ cup Budweiser® Beer

2 cups water

1 (4 oz) can sliced mushrooms, drained

1 (16 oz) can salmon, drained and flaked

2 tbsp grated Parmesan cheese

- Preheat oven to 375 degrees.
- Cook noodles according to pkg directions; drain.
- Pour noodles into 2 qt casserole.
- Add butter, sauce mix from pkg, beer, water and mushrooms.
- Place salmon over noodles.
- Cover and bake 20-25 minutes, or until casserole is bubbly.
- Remove from oven and top with almonds from pkg and Parmesan cheese.
- Serves 4.

BALLOONS RISING

Another outdoor sport, hot air ballooning, is fast gaining popularity in America, and its enthusiasts have discovered that Colorado is a "natural" for the sport.

Notwithstanding the scientific advantages of altitude, atmospheric pressure and moderate temperatures, Colorado offers a terrific array of aesthetic extras. How exhilarating to rise into a clear blue sky or an orange and lavender sunrise, and gaze down upon deep purple mountains splashed with red, gold and orange aspens, or a wavy golden wheat field, or lush green meadows, dotted with wildflowers.

Chicken Supreme

4 skinned, boneless chicken breasts
¾ cup chopped onion
2 cloves garlic, finely chopped
3 tbsp Meadow Gold Butter
1 cup sliced Rakhra Mushrooms
¾ cup water
2 tbsp white wine
Worcestershire sauce
1 tsp crushed thyme leaves
1 tsp chicken-flavor instant bouillon
1½ cups Mountain High®
Plain Yoghurt
1 egg yolk, beaten
1 tbsp all-purpose flour
½ cup red pepper strips
cooked linguine

- In skillet, brown chicken, onion and garlic in butter; add mushrooms, water, wine, Worcestershire, thyme and bouillon.
- Cover; cook 20 minutes, or until tender.
- Remove chicken; keep warm.
- Mix yoghurt, egg yolk and flour; add to skillet with red pepper. Cook and stir until thickened (do not boil).
- Serve with chicken and linguine.
- Serves 4.

TRINIDAD'S PAST

The ghosts of the Old West still haunt the streets of Trinidad.

Covered wagons passed by, pointed west, following the endless plains of the Santa Fe Trail. Doc Holliday came to the town to gamble. Billy the Kid walked the back alleys of Trinidad. So did the Black Jack Ketchum Gang. Bat Masterson even served as town marshall in a time when there was very little law and almost no order.

A glimpse of life in those early days can be found in the historic Baca House, the Bloom House, and the Pioneer Museum, all overlooking the last vestiges of the Santa Fe Trail.

Pork Meatballs Stroganoff

1 lb Cedaredge Ground Pork
½ cup soft bread crumbs
1 egg, beaten
1 tsp salt
⅛ tsp pepper
2 tbsp vegetable oil
1 cup fresh mushrooms, cut into quarters
1 small onion, chopped
1 tbsp all-purpose flour
½ cup dry sherry
½ cup water
½ cup Meadow Gold Sour Cream
hot cooked Nona Morelli Noodles
snipped parsley (optional)

- In mixing bowl, combine ground pork, bread crumbs, egg, salt and pepper; mix well.
- Shape into 12 meatballs.
- In large skillet, brown meatballs in hot oil; remove.
- Pour off pan drippings, reserving 2 tbsp in skillet.
- Cook mushrooms and onion in drippings 3 minutes, or until tender.
- Add flour; cook and stir 1-2 minutes, or until thickened and bubbly.
- Stir in sherry and water.
- Return meatballs to skillet. Simmer, covered, 20 minutes.
- Remove from heat; stir in sour cream.
- Serve over hot cooked noodles.
- Sprinkle with parsley, if desired.
- Serves 4.

TRIP OF SORROW

It was a time of sadness.

The Ute Indians had been ushered into a small corner of the state, and settlers were demanding that the tribe be removed totally from the state. In 1881, the U.S. Cavalry escorted the Uncompahgre Utes out of Colorado, moving them toward a reservation in Utah. The forced exodus would be known forever as the "Trip of Sorrow."

Some of the Indians set the land ablaze as they departed, and those settlers, waiting to claim the abandoned acreage, called the Utes' last act, "Indian Fire."

The "Indian Fire" nature trail winds through the pinon-juniper forests of Crawford State Recreation Area south of Paonia, traversing a sacred land that had been the tribe's last homeland.

Fettuccine with Mussels, Mushrooms and Romano Cheese

3 tbsp olive oil

1 lb Rakhra Mushrooms, trimmed and thinly sliced

2 large tomatoes, peeled, seeded and chopped into ½" cubes

¼ tsp nutmeg

1 (15 oz) can Dowling's Mussels Sailor Style Soup

1 lb Pasta Pasta Pasta Fettuccine

salt and freshly ground black pepper

1 cup grated Romano cheese

¼ cup finely chopped Bellwether Farms Parsley

- For sauce, heat olive oil in large skillet; add mushrooms, and cook until lightly browned.
- Add tomatoes, nutmeg and mussel soup.
- Cook over high heat 4-5 minutes.
- Remove from heat and set aside.
- Cook fettuccine "al dente"; drain, and return to pot.
- Add salt and pepper to taste, then sauce and half the cheese.
- Toss well and transfer quickly to serving bowl.
- Add remaining cheese and parsley.
- Serve immediately.
- Serves 4-6.

CODY'S GRAVE

William F. Cody is buried in Colorado, high up on Lookout Mountain west of Denver, which provides a scenic resting place for this man of action who lived out his childhood dreams. He was put to rest with an impressive funeral at which 25,000 people turned out to say good-bye. The Denver *Times* reported several months after the funeral: "The body of Buffalo Bill rests in its mountain grave, which in the years to come will be the pilgrimage of a nation." And so it is today, with an exit off of the interstate highway proclaiming Buffalo Bill's Grave. Travelers still flock to pay tribute to this American hero.

Sliced Eggs 'N Noodles

1 (7 oz) pkg noodles with chicken dinner
2 tbsp Royal Crest Butter
1 cup water
½ cup Busch® Beer
4 eggs, hard boiled and sliced
1 (5 oz) can water chestnuts, drained and diced
1 (4 oz) can sliced mushrooms, drained

- Cook noodles according to pkg directions; drain well when tender.
- Mix noodles with butter.
- In saucepan, combine sauce mix from pkg with water and beer.
- Simmer, stirring, 8-10 minutes.
- Fold in eggs, water chestnuts and mushrooms.
- Reheat until bubbly.
- Serve sauce over noodles.
- Serves 4.

Chili Mac and Cheese Casserole for Kids

1 (7.25 oz) pkg macaroni and cheese dinner
1 (15 oz) jar Championship Recipe Chili No Beans

- Prepare macaroni and cheese dinner according to pkg directions.
- When ready, mix in chili.
- Warm thoroughly; serve immediately.
- Serves 4-6.

THE COMING OF WHITE GOLD

At first, the color of Breckenridge was gold.

By 1860, there were more than 8,000 honest, solid citizens living in cabins, tents and shanties that lined Main Street, all digging the good earth for nuggets that would make them rich overnight.

By 1880, the boom town boasted eighteen saloons and three dance halls. During the next two decades, however, the mineral deposits were depleted in the mountains around Breckenridge, and its population dropped below one thousand.

After World War II, it had virtually become a ghost town.

But Breckenridge discovered the value of snow, and today it is one of Colorado's world class skiing resorts.

The ski trails traverse three mountains, and the landscape also features cross-country skiing, ice skating, sleigh rides, and snowmobiling. Breckenridge is still aglitter. But the color has changed from gold to white.

Meat Ravioli with Garlic and Olive Oil

1 pkg Frangi's Mini-Meat Ravioli
2 tbsp olive oil
2 cups chopped fresh garlic
1 Rosey Farms Red Pepper, sliced
1 cup grated Romano cheese

- Prepare ravioli according to pkg directions; drain and set aside.
- Add olive oil to pan over medium heat.
- Sauté garlic and red pepper in oil.
- Add cooked ravioli to pan; heat thoroughly until done.
- Remove from pan, and toss with cheese.
- Serves 4-6.

"GO WEST, YOUNG MAN"

Nathan Meeker, the agricultural editor of the *New York Times*, journeyed west and was inspired by the grandeur of Colorado. He promptly devised a plan to create a "western colony," basing it on the principles of religion, temperance, education, agriculture, irrigation and cooperation.

Horace Greeley gave his approval, and Meeker's story on the western colony appeared in the December 1869 issue of the *New York Times*. He encouraged temperance and individuals with money to write him if they had any interest in becoming part of the colony. He expected few replies. Thousands wrote, and fifty-nine of them paid $155 each for a membership in the Union Colony. In time, seven hundred joined. And they trekked together to Colorado, founding a town that Nathan Meeker named Greeley for his mentor and benefactor at the *New York Times*, Horace Greely. After all, it was Greeley who had proclaimed, "Go west, young man."

Fresh Tomato Sauce with Pesto

1 lb Roma tomatoes, thickly sliced
2 tbsp olive oil
1 (6 oz) ctn Chapin's Supreme Basil or Sun-Dried Tomato Pesto
cooked Pastarific Garlic Parsley Fettuccine
grated Parmesan cheese

• Sauté tomatoes in olive oil for 2 minutes.
• Remove from heat; stir in pesto.
• Serve over hot fettuccine. Sprinkle with Parmesan cheese.
• Serves 4.

COLORADO: BOOM AND BUST

You cannot escape Colorado's boom and bust cycle. First skins and buffalo, then gold, then silver, then less precious but still valuable ores, then health spas, later uranium and oil, now outdoor sports. Each in its time has made men wealthy off the land, and, except for today's boom cycle, each has gone bust.

For many residents life has not been easy. What motivates these people to remain in this land when the elements often seem to conspire against them? Each person has his or her own answer, but there are some common threads:

The awesome natural beauty, which is as close as your front window or within a reasonable drive in any direction. It may be moonlight on a canyon's sheer walls or a herd of Pronghorn's greeting the dawn on the Front Range, or a small lake set against the San Juans or the white stillness of the morning after a blizzard. The list is as endless as nature itself. For this is forever a land of mountains and deserts and trees and streams.

La Dolce Ziti

⅓ lb ziti

1 zucchini, sliced or 1 yellow squash, sliced

2 cups diced cooked Bar-S Ham

¾ cup baby green peas

½ cup Graves Dairy Half and Half

1 (15 oz) ctn Chapin's Supreme Pepperonata Sauce

grated Parmesan cheese

- Cook ziti according to pkg directions; drain and pour into casserole dish.
- Add sliced zucchini or yellow squash, ham, green peas, cream and pepperonata sauce.
- Top with cheese; microwave 15 minutes, or until vegetables are crisp tender and cheese is bubbly.
- Serves 4.

WHERE THE WIND BLOWS FREE

Perhaps no one ever described the mystique, the spirit of Colorado more eloquently than did Ten Bears, a Yamparike Comanche chieftain in 1860. He said: "I was born upon the prairie, where the wind blew free and there was nothing to break the light of the sun."

Ravioli Parmigana

1 pkg Frangi's Jumbo Ravioli Cheese, Sausage or Beef
2 cups Frangi's Spaghetti Sauce
2 cups grated Leprino Mozzerella Cheese
¼ cup grated Romano cheese

- Preheat oven to 375 degrees.
- Parboil ravioli 6-7 minutes.
- Layer spaghetti sauce in bottom of 9″ x 9″ baking dish.
- Add layer of ravioli.
- Top with more spaghetti sauce.
- Layer mozzerella on top; sprinkle with Romano cheese.
- Bake 20-25 minutes.
- Serves 6-8.

Spinach Ravioli Alfredo

1 pkg Frangi's Jumbo Spinach Ravioli
1 cup Robinson Butter
1 (8 oz) pkg cream cheese, softened
2 cups Robinson Heavy Cream
¼ cup cooking sherry
¼ tsp nutmeg
2 tsp white pepper
½ tsp salt
1 cup grated Parmesan cheese, divided

- Cook spinach ravioli according to pkg directions; drain and set aside.
- Combine butter, cream cheese, cream, sherry, nutmeg, white pepper and salt.
- Cook over low heat until blended and smooth.
- Remove sauce from heat; stir in ½ cup cheese.
- Top ravioli with sauce; sprinkle on remaining cheese.
- Serves 4-6.

SECLUDED SPOTS

It comes on you slowly, that sense that you are alone with all of the beauty of Colorado as you rest under the shade of a tree deep in the high country or Colorado's Eastern "Outback". You may find evidence that man has been here before, or maybe nothing will break the feeling that this spot is yours alone. There are many of these places throughout the state. You cannot find them by driving. You will need to walk or ski or mount a horse and ride to them. Once you have found your spot you will always know it. The Indians and miners and soldiers and farmers and businessmen of past eras also found such spots. The remote beauty of these places spurred people such as Kit Carson and Jim Bridger to want to stay and live in these mountains. The spots are still there for you to find and love, right here and right now in Colorado.

Frankly Noodle Casserole

1 (6 oz) pkg Italian noodle dinner

1 (8 oz) ctn Meadow Gold Creamed Cottage Cheese

4 Longmont Turkey Frankfurters, cut into thin slices

½ cup Michelob® Beer

1 cup water

2 tbsp grated Parmesan cheese

- Preheat oven to 350 degrees.
- Cook noodles from mix according to pkg directions; drain well when tender.
- Place half the noodles in well buttered 1½ qt casserole.
- Sprinkle cheese mix from pkg over noodles.
- Spoon cottage cheese evenly over noodles.
- Top with remaining noodles and franks.
- Combine tomato sauce mix from pkg, beer and water.
- Pour mixture evenly over casserole.
- Sprinkle top with Parmesan cheese.
- Bake 25-30 minutes, or until casserole is bubbly.
- Serves 4.

MAIN DISHES

Pawnee Buttes, Pawnee National Grassland

Photo by Jeff Andrew

CROSSING THE ROYAL GORGE

Although Zebulon Pike was a great explorer, he had no faith in his fellow man. He looked at the peak that would bear his name and swore that no one would ever ascend it. A road now climbs to the top. Then Pike stood on the ridges above Royal Gorge and predicted that no one would ever cross it. But then, Pike would never know about the daring, the ingenuity of Lon Piper, a bridge builder, who, in 1929, figured out a way to place the world's highest suspension bridge across the gorge, a jagged gash by the Rio Grande river, 1,200 feet into the earth near Cañon City. An aerial tramway also eases silently across the Royal Gorge. And you can either take an incline railway to the bottom or ride horseback on a guided tour down a narrow trail that winds along the canyon walls. Below, the whitewater rafters challenge the rapids of Sunshine Falls, Mount Rush, the Sledge Hammer, and the Corkscrew.

Saguache Stir-Fry

¼ lb Life Force Chinese Bean Sprouts
1 carrot
2 cups fresh pea pods
½ head cabbage
½ head purple cabbage
½ onion
¼ lb Rakhra Mushrooms
10 tbsp teriyaki sauce
1 lb Coleman Natural Beef Top Sirloin
¼ cup Marsala wine (optional)
cooked rice

- Chop vegetables into bite-size pieces.
- Heat wok to 400 degrees.
- Sear wok with 2 tbsp teriyaki sauce.
- Brown meat with wine and 4 tbsp teriyaki sauce for 5 minutes.
- Add vegetables to meat.
- Add remaining teriyaki sauce to taste.
- Simmer for 3-5 minutes.
- Serve with cooked rice.
- Serves 6.

VALLEY OF SPRINGS

James Crawford brought his family into a land cobwebbed with hot springs where, according to Indian legend, the Great Spirit lived deep below the surface of the earth. There were more than 150 springs with names such as Bird's Nest, Fairy Lake, Frying Pan, Aeolian, Annie, Baby and Hades. The hot mineral water became the great attraction for the health resort of Steamboat Springs. As Dr. R.E. Jones said: "Mineral springs are magical in their charm for man. All people have an abiding faith in nature and the mysterious workings that are constantly taking place in her unseen laboratories deep below the earth's surface. Many feel that she is dispensing chemical combinations far beyond the possibility of man to so."

Spanish Beef and Squash Supreme

1 onion, chopped

2 cloves garlic, minced, divided

1 tsp vegetable oil

2 lbs Maverick Ranch NaturaLite Beef Ground Chuck

2 cups sliced yellow crook neck squash

½ cup grated Parmesan cheese

½ cup grated Monterey Jack cheese

½ cup Golden Peaks Lowfat Milk

⅔ cup dry whole wheat bread crumbs

1 tbsp minced parsley or parsley flakes

2 eggs, beaten

½ tsp oregano

¼ tsp salt

⅛ tsp pepper

1 (4 oz) can chopped green chilies

½ cup grated Cheddar cheese

- In skillet, brown onion, and 1 minced garlic clove in oil until clear.
- Add ground chuck and cook until light pink in color, remove from pan to bowl; set aside.
- In large covered pan, boil squash with remaining minced garlic clove in water to cover; drain.
- In medium bowl, mix Parmesan, Monterey Jack, milk, bread crumbs, parsley, eggs, oregano, salt and pepper. Fold in green chilies.
- Gently combine with beef and squash mixture in large baking dish. Top with Cheddar cheese.
- Bake at 325 degrees 25-30 minutes.
- Serves 4-6.

AROUND COLORADO SPRINGS

In the Colorado Springs area are Pikes Peak, the Garden of the Gods, the Cave of the Winds and the North Pole, home of Santa's Workshop. Additionally, you will be close to the internationally famous Royal Gorge which boasts the world's highest suspension bridge, 1,053 feet above the railroad and the Arkansas River.

One of the jewels of the U.S. military also exists here. The U.S. Air Force Academy is located just outside the Springs. An excellent Visitor's Center provides interested parties with extensive information. The Academy hosts nearly one million visitors each year.

Buffalo with Broccoli Stir-Fry

⅓ cup soy sauce

2 tbsp cider vinegar

¾ tsp sugar

1 cube beef bouillon

⅓ cup water

4 tsp cornstarch

3 tbsp peanut oil

2 large cloves garlic, crushed

1 lb sirloin or top round Lay Valley Bison Ranch Buffalo Steak, sliced into ⅛" strips

1 large Tateys Onion, chopped

1½ cups broccoli stems, sliced into ⅛" diagonal strips

2½ cups Charley Hayashida Broccoli Flowerets

¼ lb fresh mushrooms, sliced

Denver To-Fu Chinese Noodles

- Mix together soy sauce, vinegar and sugar; set aside.
- In another container, mix bouillon, water and cornstarch.
- In wok or heavy large skillet add 1½ tbsp peanut oil over high heat.
- Add garlic and meat; stir-fry for 2 minutes, or until medium brown and pink in center.
- Remove meat and pan juices. Add 1 tbsp peanut oil.
- When oil is hot, add onion and broccoli stems; stir-fry 2 minutes, until crisp and tender.
- Add remaining oil around edge of wok; add broccoli and mushrooms; stir-fry 2 minutes.
- Pour in meat, juices, soy sauce, vinegar and sugar mixture. Stir, cover and cook 2 minutes.
- Stir cornstarch mixture; pour into wok, stirring constantly 2-3 minutes, until thickened.
- Serve over Chinese noodles.
- Serves 4.

COLORADO'S TOP ATTRACTION

Through the years, the United States Air Force Academy in Colorado Springs has become the state's most visited man-made attraction. At the Academy, situated regally at the foot of the majestic Rampart Mountains, you can visit the beautiful all-faith Cadet Chapel, which features seventeen 150-foot spires, the planetarium, and the USAFA Visitors Center.

Four Corners Rabbitchiladas

1 (10.5 oz) can cream of chicken soup

1 (10.5 oz) can cream of mushroom soup

1 medium OGI Onion, grated

1 doz La Tolteca Corn Tortillas, shredded

1 cup chopped jalapeno peppers

1 lb Bar-S Colby Sharp Cheese, grated

2 small Four Corners Fryer Rabbit, cooked and choped

Salsa:

2 tbsp vegetable oil

1 cup diced onion

1 cup diced celery

1 cup sliced carrots

3 cloves garlic, minced

1½ cups chopped hot peppers

1 tbsp dried parsley

1 tbsp dried cilantro

4 cups Cream of the Valley Tomato Puree

½ cup wine vinegar

1 tsp salt

1 tsp sugar

- Combine soups and onion.
- In 11½" x 7½" glass baking dish, layer tortillas, soup mixture, peppers, cheese and rabbit.
- Bake in 350 degree oven 30 minutes.
- For salsa, in large saucepan, heat oil; add onion, celery, carrots, garlic and peppers.
- Sauté until soft.
- Add parsley, cilantro, puree, vinegar, salt and sugar.
- Simmer 45 minutes.
- Allow to cool slightly; blend in food processor until smooth.
- Return to saucepan; heat and simmer 20 minutes.
- Spoon over rabbitchiladas before serving.
- Serves 6-8.

ARCHITECTURAL PERFECTION

The Manitou Cliff Dwellings look down upon the Victorian town of Manitou Springs. They are the mysterious remains of an Indian culture that thrived from 1100 to 1300 A.D. There are more than forty rooms in the pueblo, including a ceremonial Kiva, look-out tower and sleeping quarters. A garden also points out how the Taos Pueblo Indians depended on the plants that grew throughout their homeland. From the narrow leaf yucca, they made sandals and baskets. Tips of the plant were fashioned into needles and paint brushes. And the leaves were bundled and tied together to form brooms and chair brushes. Leaves from the broadleaf yucca were shredded and twisted into rope. And soap, made from its crushed roots, was used as shampoo.

Beef Tenderloin with Vegetable Medley

3 tbsp butter

4 Colorado Beef Tenderloin Steaks, 1¼" thick

1 (6 oz) jar marinated artichokes, reserving marinade liquid

2 medium Rosey Farms Tomatoes, chopped

1 (4 oz) can sliced mushrooms

1 tsp Colorado Spice Co. Lemon Pepper

1 tbsp capers

2 tbsp chopped green onions

cooked wild rice

- In heavy 10" skillet, melt butter.
- When skillet is heated, add steaks; cook, uncovered, over medium high heat 4 minutes.
- Turn over when browned; cook 3-4 minutes more.
- Transfer to serving platter; keep warm while preparing vegetables.
- Add reserved artichoke liquid to skillet. Stir to combine with residue in skillet; lower heat.
- Add artichokes, tomatoes and mushrooms. Sprinkle with lemon pepper; heat thoroughly.
- Top each tenderloin with a portion of vegetable mixture.
- Garnish with capers and green onions.
- Serve with wild rice.
- Serves 4.

A GOLDEN BIRTHRIGHT

On a warm afternoon in August, back in 1859, a band of fourteen prospectors, led by General George E. Spencer, knelt beside the Blue River and promptly made the first recorded discovery of gold on Colorado's western slope.

There was no reason for them to travel any further into the mountains, so they built a log and sod fortification that became the foundation for a town.

The prospectors had to call their village something. So they named it after John C. Breckinridge, the vice president of the United States. None of them knew the vice president, but they thought using his name might help them get a post office, and, perhaps, it did. However, when the vice president received his commission as a Confederate officer, the angry Unionists quickly changed the town's name to "Breckenridge," replacing the "i" with an "e".

Pulkogi

1 tsp sesame seed

1 lb Colorado Beef Sirloin Steak, thinly sliced into 2"-3" strips

4 green onions, chopped

3 tbsp GW Granulated Sugar

1 tbsp soy sauce

1 tsp sesame oil

1 tsp Colorado Spice Co. Garlic Powder

vegetable oil

cooked rice

- Toast sesame seeds in shallow pan in 350 degree oven 10-12 minutes, until lightly browned. Shake often to prevent burning.

- Combine all ingredients and marinate at least 1 hour or overnight. Do not drain.

- Stir-fry until done in heavy skillet or wok with small amount of oil. Prepare just before serving.

- Serve with rice.

- Serves 4.

The Healy House, Leadville

Photo by Jeff Andrew

HAPPY VALENTINE'S DAY

On February 14 of each year, Loveland is the most popular city in the United States. The post office receives hundreds of thousands of valentines to be remailed with a special cachet and the Loveland postmark. After all, Loveland refers to itself as "Cupid's Hometown, the Valentine Capital of the World."

Crawfish Etoufee

8 green peppers, chopped
1 stalk celery, chopped
2 onions, chopped
4 tbsp butter
3 tbsp minced garlic
1 tbsp thyme
3 bay leaves
2½ cups sliced green onions
5 tbsp Lucile's Creole Seasoning
2 tsp hot pepper sauce
3 tbsp Worcestershire sauce
13 cups fish stock
¼ cup tomato puree
1 cup butter
3 lbs crawfish tail meat or shelled shrimp
8 cups cooked rice

Brown Roux:
½ cup vegetable oil
1 cup all-purpose flour

- To make brown roux, heat oil for about 1 minute in heavy skillet; stir in flour with wooden spoon until smooth.
- Continue cooking until roux is medium brown, 1-2 minutes, stirring to prevent burning or scorching. Remove from heat and reserve.
- In large stock pot, sauté peppers, celery and onions in butter until cooked thoroughly.
- Add next 9 ingredients and stir well to blend; bring to boil.
- Add roux, butter and crawfish or shrimp; stir and cook until fish is cooked.
- Serve hot over cooked rice.
- Serves 15-20.

BUFFALO BILL: THE EARLY DAYS

Buffalo Bill Cody is a name synonomous with the West and particularly Colorado. President Theodore Roosevelt called him "an American of Americans." He was the youngest wagon master and the youngest Pony Express rider on record. And, concerning the latter, he made one continuous ride of twenty-four hours and forty minutes, going three hundred twenty-two miles and using twenty-one horses.

How did Cody get the name Buffalo Bill? From 1867 to 1868 he gained his first public notice as a buffalo hunter by supplying meat for the Kansas Pacific Railroad. He hunted only for food and gained his famous name by shooting a record 4,289 buffalo in one season. That was used to feed over 1,000 track layers for the railroad.

Cashew Pork Stir-Fry

1 tbsp grated orange rind
¾ cup Marquest Orange Juice
1 tbsp cornstarch
3 tbsp soy sauce
⅓ cup corn syrup
¼ tsp ginger
2 tbsp vegetable oil, divided
2 large carrots, peeled and sliced diagonally
2 stalks celery, sliced diagonally
1 lb Colorado Pork Tenderloin, cut into thin strips
½ cup Bennett Cashews
cooked rice (optional)

- Combine first 6 ingredients, stirring well.
- Heat 1 tbsp oil in large skillet over medium heat.
- Add carrots and celery, stir-frying about 3 minutes.
- Remove vegetables, set aside.
- Pour remaining tbsp oil into skillet.
- Add pork, stir-frying 3 minutes.
- Return vegetables to pan, add orange juice mixture and cashews.
- Cook, stirring constantly, over medium high heat, until thickened.
- Serve over hot rice, if desired.
- Serves 4.

BUFFALO BILL: THE SHOWMAN

Buffalo Bill was a guide, horseman, hunter, stagecoach driver and army scout. But his fame began when he met Ned Buntline, who brought his exploits to the attention of others through his dime novels and dramas. Cody's appearance at the dramas was the only thing required to turn out huge audiences.

From 1883 to 1913 Buffalo Bill led his Wild West show across the nation and around the world. It made more than $1 million a year and featured over 640 cowboys and Indians as well as one of the largest buffalo herds in existence. Mark Twain wrote of the show: "down to its smallest details, the show is genuine . . . it is wholly free from sham and insincerity." Buffalo Bill's best-known star was Phoebe Ann Moses, better known by her stage name of Annie Oakley.

Ribs 'N Rice

1½ lbs Colorado Beef Spareribs

2 tbsp butter

1 (7 oz) pkg ham flavored rice and vermicelli

1 cup water

1 cup Budweiser® Beer

¼ cup vinegar

1 (8 oz) can pineapple chunks

- Preheat oven to 350 degrees.
- Cut spareribs into individual pieces; brown slowly on all sides in skillet 30 minutes.
- Remove ribs.
- Add butter to skillet; brown rice mixture until golden.
- Add water, beer and vinegar.
- Cook, covered, until liquid is absorbed and rice is tender, about 20 minutes.
- Stir pineapple chunks and juice into rice.
- Put half the rice into bottom of 2 qt casserole.
- Place ribs on top and cover with remaining rice. Cover casserole.
- Bake in oven 40 minutes.
- Serves 4.

A GREAT STATE FAIR

A traditional place for getting a feel for the agricultural products of a state is the State Fair. Colorado is no exception. Its State Fair is one of the state's most exciting festivals. As in other states, Colorado's fair was originally staged as an event to celebrate the bounty of its agriculture and thus set up competitions for judging the best products.

Colorado's fair has been held in Pueblo, in southern Colorado, since before statehood. As a major transportation hub, as well as field crop and vegetable-growing region in early years, the location was a natural choice. The fairgrounds are located in the southwest corner of the city; signs on Interstate 25 mark the appropriate exits. The fair attracts about 750,000 visitors annually, and generates some $40 million for the local economy.

Stir-Fry Chinese Rabbit

1 Four Corners Fryer Rabbit
2 tbsp cornstarch
2 tbsp sherry
2 tbsp soy sauce
4 tbsp peanut oil
1 medium green pepper, sliced
¼ lb fresh mushrooms, sliced
8 water chestnuts, sliced
2 tbsp F & J Worcestershire Sauce
¼ cup sliced Naturally Nuts Cashews
cooked rice

- Debone rabbit; cut into small strips.
- Mix cornstarch, sherry and soy sauce.
- Marinate rabbit for 24 hours.
- Put wok or skillet over high heat.
- Add 2 tbsp oil, green peppers, mushrooms and chestnuts; stir-fry 2 minutes; remove from wok and reserve.
- Add remaining oil and rabbit to wok.
- Return vegetables to wok, add Worcestershire sauce and nuts.
- Cook 2 minutes; serve over rice.
- Serves 4.

4-Way Grilled Cheese

4 tsp margarine

8 slices Earth Grains Very Thin Wheat Bread

4 tsp Colorado Spice Co. Sesame Seeds

1 green bell pepper, thinly sliced into rings

4 (1 oz) slices Cheddar cheese

4 (1 oz) slices Banes Ham

1 red bell pepper, thinly sliced into rings

4 (1 oz) slices Monterey Jack cheese

- Spread ½ tsp margarine on 1 side of each bread slice.
- Sprinkle ½ tsp sesame seeds on each slice, pressing lightly with fingers so seeds adhere.
- To assemble each sandwich, place 1 bread slice buttered side down.
- Add 2 green pepper rings, 1 slice Cheddar cheese, 1 slice ham, 2 red pepper rings, 1 slice Monterey Jack cheese; top with second bread slice, buttered side up.
- Grill sandwiches 4-5 minutes, or until cheese is melted and seeds are light golden.
- Serves 4.

Pork Chop and Potato Casserole

3-4 medium Martins Leader Potatoes, thinly sliced

1 onion, thinly sliced

4-6 Banes Pork Chops, browned

salt and pepper

garlic salt

1 (10.5 oz) can cream of mushroom soup

½ soup can Graves Dairy Milk

- Place potatoes in greased casserole; arrange onions on top.
- Place pork chops on top of potatoes and onions.
- Season potatoes and pork chops with salt, pepper and garlic salt to taste.
- Mix the soup with milk; pour over casserole ingredients.
- Bake 1 hour in 350 degree oven.
- Serves 4.

COMMERCE ON THE SANTA FE TRAIL

Bent's Old Fort served as a commercial crossroads in southeastern Colorado. Trade goods were hauled along the Santa Fe Trail. Indian tribes—the Cheyenne, Arapaho, Ute, Northern Apache, Kiowa and Comanche—brought in buffalo robes. And mountain men came to barter their beaver pelts.

In 1840, a trader wrote of it: "Although built of the simple prairie soil, made to hold together by a rude mixture with straw and the plain grass itself . . . (Bent's Old Fort) is constructed with all the defensive capacities of a complete fortification. The dwellings, the kitchens, the arrangements for comfort are all such as to strike the wanderer with the liveliest surprise, as though an 'air-built castle' had dropped to earth before him in the midst of a vast desert."

Bent's Old Fort, reconstructed near La Junta, is now a National Historic Site where costumed interpreters escort you back into the unpredictable days of the 1830s.

Chicken Santa Fe

2½ lbs Banes Chicken Breasts, chopped

1 cup rice

1 (15 oz) ctn Chapin's Supreme Green Chili Sauce

½ cup water

1 cup frozen peas

1 cup frozen corn

tomato, green onions or artichoke hearts (optional)

- Brown chicken pieces in non-stick pan.
- Remove chicken and sauté rice. Add chili sauce, chicken and water; cover and bake at 350 degrees 30 minutes.
- Fold in peas and corn; bake 10 more minutes.
- Just before serving, add tomato, green onions or artichoke hearts, if desired.
- Serves 4-6.

TOPS IN THE WEST

The "Stetson" hat, revered throughout the history of the West, had its beginnings in the mining camp of Central City. It seems John B. Stetson was headed west to find a cure for tuberculosis, a common disease among hatters. While encamped one night he showed companions how to process fur without tanning. For amusement, Stetson then created a hat which looked odd, but was considered the best thing for the Colorado weather. He continued to wear the hat as he traveled, until one day in Central City a horseman asked to try the hat on and then bought it immediately. Thus was the famous "Boss of the Plains" hat launched.

Garden Stir-Fry

1 lb White Wave Tofu, cut into 1" cubes
2 tbsp vegetable oil
2 cups water
⅓ cup soy sauce
2¼ tbsp cornstarch
2 onions, thinly sliced
2 tbsp vegetable oil
1 cup sliced mushrooms
1 cup Bennett Walnut Halves
2 Piedmont Farms Carrots, thinly sliced
2 cups Piedmont Farms Broccoli Tops
cooked Nona Morelli Pasta

- Brown tofu lightly in oil.
- Blend water, soy sauce and cornstarch; set aside.
- Over medium heat, sauté onions in oil until transparent; add remaining ingredients.
- Increase heat to medium high. Stir; add tofu and blended sauce, cooking until hot, 5-10 minutes.
- Serve over pasta or rice.
- Serves 4.

MOST FAMOUS WOMAN

The saga of Colorado is not that of man alone, for women played significant roles throughout its history. Helen Hunt Jackson was one of them. Once called the most famous woman to live in Colorado, she was an avid writer and the author of the famous novel *Ramona*. She lived in Colorado Springs in a fine home built by a carpenter named Winfield Scott Stratton, who later became the first Cripple Creek gold millionaire. However, before *Ramona*, Mrs. Jackson prepared a study of the U.S. Government's dealings with the Indians entitled *A Century of Dishonor*. It was a massive indictment of the official policies regarding the Indians. She was reviled, but later became a Commissioner of Indian Affairs. During her travels related to the position, she became inspired to write *Ramona*, which was considered to be one of the two great ethical novels of the century.

Sauer-Hot Dogs

4 Bar-S Beef Franks

4 (.5 oz) sticks extra sharp Cheddar cheese

4 slices Earth Grains Very Thin Sandwich White Bread

1 cup sauerkraut, well drained

4 tsp brown mustard

- Preheat oven to 375 degrees.
- Make lengthwise cut in each frank; insert cheese stick.
- Place franks in small non-stick pan.
- Cover each frank with ¼ cup sauerkraut, pressing firmly around frank.
- Spread 1 tsp mustard on each bread slice.
- Fold bread slices over franks, blanket style.
- Place close together so bread edges do not pop up.
- Bake 20 minutes, or until heated thoroughly.
- To serve, remove from pan and turn over; bread will form a hot dog "roll."
- Serves 4.

FROM SILVER TO SKIS

A one-time silver town, Aspen was originally named "Ute City" and had its origins in 1879. It thrived during the silver era, but began to decline when silver prices dropped in 1893. However, in the 1930's Aspen began a regeneration as a ski resort. It continues today as an international skiing destination for many and a home for the rich and famous, far from the crowds in their centers of business. The Hotel Jerome, Wheeler Opera House and other historic sites provide the visitor with ample opportunity to learn about the past and present, if they do not wish to try their hand at the slopes. The drive into Aspen from either direction takes the traveler through such scenic wonders as Independence Pass or along the banks of the Roaring Fork River and through the sheer canyon walls leading into Glenwood Springs.

Stuffed Pork Chops with Mushroom Gravy

1 (8 oz) pkg cornbread stuffing mix
½ cup butter
1 onion, chopped
⅓ cup finely chopped celery
½ cup Michelob® Beer
1 egg, well beaten
6 thick, center cut Cedaredge Pork Chops, slashed to form a pocket
1 (1 oz) pkg mushroom gravy mix
½ cup water
½ cup Michelob® Beer
pinch crumbled sage

- Preheat oven to 350 degrees.
- Combine stuffing mix, butter, onion, celery, beer and egg; blend well.
- Stuff pocket in pork chops with mixture.
- Shape remaining stuffing into small balls.
- Place pork chops in single layer in shallow baking pan.
- Bake in oven 1 hour, or until pork chops are easily pierced.
- Stuffing balls should be added 30 minutes before pork chops are done.
- In saucepan, combine remaining ingredients; cook, stirring constantly, until sauce bubbles and thickens.
- Place chops and stuffing balls on serving plates and spoon sauce over chops.
- Serves 6.

GOLDEN: MORE THAN A BREWERY

Each year thousands of visitors come to Golden, Colorado to spend time touring the Coors brewery, which is still on the site of Adolph Coors' first brewery. But Golden is more than just the brewery. It's the home of the highly respected Colorado School of Mines, the Colorado Railroad Museum, the School of Mines Geology Museum and a Fine Art Center that features regional arts and crafts.

Golden was briefly the capital of Colorado and a banner across its main street reads "Where the West Remains." Also nestled in this distinctive little community is one of the areas finest restaurants, The Briarwood Inn.

Mrs. Coors' Sauerbraten

1 (12 oz) can Coors Beer	• Combine first 10 ingredients.
1½ cups red wine vinegar	• Place roast in plastic bag; set in shallow pan.
2 medium onions, sliced	
1 lemon, sliced	• Pour marinade over roast; close bag.
12 whole cloves	• Refrigerate 72 hours, turning occasionally.
6 whole black peppercorns, crushed	
4 bay leaves, crushed	• Remove roast; pat dry.
1 tbsp sugar	• Strain marinade; set aside.
¼ tsp ginger	• Brown roast in hot oil; drain drippings.
1 tbsp salt	
1 (4 lb) boneless beef rump roast	• Add reserved marinade, chopped onion, carrot and celery.
2 tbsp vegetable oil	• Cover; simmer 2 hours or until roast is tender; remove roast.
½ cup chopped onion	
½ cup chopped carrot	• Reserve 2 cups cooking liquid and vegetables.
¼ cup chopped celery	
1 cup crushed gingersnaps	• Stir in gingersnaps and water; cook and stir until thickened.
⅔ cup water	• Serve with roast and noodles.
hot buttered noodles	• Serves 12.

© Meredith Corporation 1981.

DENVER'S NEXT BOOM

Founded in 1858 at the confluence of Cherry Creek and the Platte River, Denver was only a stop along the way to the gold fields at first. Later, when the railroads arrived, it began its true development. Today, it is a regional hub for government, transportation, distribution and industry.

To the visitor, must see sights abound, such as the State Capitol building, the U.S. Mint, Museum of Western Art, Denver Fire Fighters Museum, Larimer Square, the Governor's Mansion and on and on.

Shrimp and Scallop Sauté

½ lb medium Keeton Fisheries Shrimp, peeled and cleaned

½ lb fresh large scallops, quartered

salt and pepper

2 tbsp butter, divided

2 tsp chopped shallots

4 tsp sliced green onions

1 lb Rakhra Mushrooms, sliced

⅛ tsp cayenne

1 tsp paprika

1 (15 oz) can Dowling's Mussels Sailor Style Soup

cooked rice, toast points or pastry shells

2 tbsp chopped parsley to garnish

- Season shrimp and scallops with salt and pepper.
- Heat large skillet or wok; add half the butter.
- When butter is hot, add shrimp and scallops.
- Cook until lightly browned, but slightly underdone; remove to heated platter.
- Wipe out skillet or wok and return to heat.
- Add remaining butter and sauté shallots, green onions and mushrooms 2 minutes.
- Return shrimp, scallops and their juices to skillet or wok.
- Add cayenne, paprika and soup.
- Bring back to a simmer; season to taste.
- Serve on individual plates on rice, toast points or pastry shells.
- Garnish with parsley.
- Serves 4-6.

IRRIGATING COLORADO

Irrigation activities in Colorado began during the 1870s and 1880s. Developers built canals and reservoirs along major rivers. Before the turn of the century the systems were overloaded. There simply was not enough water to supply them. The next logical step was to sink wells. Later, projects were developed to bring Western Slope water through the mountains to the Eastern Plains. River diversion projects also came into vogue, but the extensive use of these systems created another problem—water rights. To this day that legal battle is still joined. Irrigation continues extensively in the state today, but not unopposed.

Taco Dogs

1 (16 oz) pkg Bar-S Jumbo Franks
8 hot dog buns
1 (10 oz) can chili hot dog sauce
1 cup shredded Cheddar cheese
1 cup crushed Great Western Golden Rounds
shredded lettuce (optional)
chopped tomatoes (optional)

- Cover microwave plate with paper towel.
- Place 4 franks in 4 buns; put on plate.
- Spoon half the sauce over the franks; sprinkle half the cheese and crushed chips on top.
- Cover all hot dogs with waxed paper.
- Microwave on HIGH 3-4 minutes, or until cheese is melted and buns are hot to touch.
- Rotate plate half turn half way through cooking time.
- Sprinkle lightly with lettuce and tomatoes, if desired.
- Repeat steps to prepare remaining hot dogs.
- Serves 6-8.

MANY-FACETED COLORADO SPRINGS

Zebulon Pike discovered the area and General William Jackson Palmer developed it. Thus Colorado Springs had a great start at becoming an area which people would want to live in or visit. Its attractions are extensive: the Colorado Springs Pioneers Museum, the Broadmoor, Cheyenne Mountain Zoo, World Figure Skating Hall of Fame and Museum, White House Ranch, the Western Museum of Mining and Industry, the Pro Rodeo Hall of Fame and Museum of the American Cowboy, and the U.S. Olympic Training Center to name just a few.

Hot Hoagie Sandwich

½ loaf unsliced Gerard's French Bread
Rosalie's Salad Dressing
Mady's Zesty Honey Mustard
8 slices Bar-S Sliced Luncheon Meats
4 slices cheese
shredded lettuce
tomato slices
onion slices

- Cut bread lengthwise to make 2 long thin pieces.
- Spread both cut sides evenly with salad dressing and mustard.
- Cover both sides with meat slices; cover meat on bottom of loaf with cheese slices.
- Place meat covered top half of bread over bottom half.
- Wrap sandwich loosely with a paper towel and place on a microwave safe dish.
- Microwave on MEDIUM HIGH 5-7 minutes, or until meat is warm and cheese begins to melt.
- Cool slightly before slicing.
- Add lettuce, tomato and onion, if desired.
- Serves 3-4.

DENVER: STILL WESTERN

Once thought of as a town which may have already peaked, the Denver of today is moving briskly ahead through such things as a new convention center and a new international airport. Residents are seeking to make the next "boom" a continuing one by bringing in industries which can serve not only the citizens of the city and state, but many in the region.

However, despite its cosmopolitan face, Denver retains its casual, Western flavor. Let's hope that part of the city never changes.

Western-Style Hamburgers

Ingredients	Instructions
2 tbsp vegetable oil	• Heat 2 tbsp oil in medium skillet.
1 large purple onion, peeled and finely minced	• Sauté onion and garlic in oil over low heat until soft but not brown.
2 cloves garlic, peeled and finely minced	• Add chili sauce and jalapeno relish; bring to boil.
1 cup chili sauce	
1 tbsp jalapeno relish	• Lower heat; simmer 5 minutes.
½ cup brewed Boyer's Coffee	• Stir in coffee. Keep on low heat 5-10 minutes, but do not boil after adding coffee.
1 tbsp vegetable oil	
1½ lbs ground beef	• Remove from heat; keep warm.
3 Vie de France Hamburger Buns, thawed and toasted	• Heat 1 tbsp oil in large skillet.
1 cup grated sharp Cheddar cheese	• Shape meat into 6 thick patties. Brown in oil over high heat.
	• Turn patties; lower heat. Cook 5-10 minutes.
	• Place on toasted buns. Cover with hot sauce and top with cheese.
	• Serve immediately.
	• Serves 6.

Maverick Crustless Pizza

1 tbsp vegetable oil

1 medium onion, finely chopped

1½ lbs Maverick Ranch NaturaLite Beef Ground Round

2 egg whites

½ cup fine dry whole wheat bread crumbs

¾ cup Chapin's Supreme Sun-Dried Tomato Pesto

1 cup shredded Leprino Mozzarella Cheese

½ green pepper, thinly sliced into rings

½ cup sliced Rakhra Mushrooms

¼ cup sliced olives

¼ cup freshly grated Parmesan cheese

- Heat salad oil in non-stick skillet.
- Add onion and sauté until clear and browned, about 5 minutes.
- Transfer to medium bowl; add beef, egg whites and bread crumbs; mix thoroughly.
- Pat mixture into same skillet to form giant patty.
- Over medium heat, brown patty 5 minutes, shaking pan frequently to prevent sticking.
- Place baking sheet over skillet; turn out patty onto baking sheet.
- Carefully slip patty back into skillet with uncooked side down.
- Cook 5 minutes, or until desired doneness.
- Remove pan from heat; discard drippings in pan.
- Spoon sauce over patty; spread smoothly to edges.
- Sprinkle with mozzarella cheese.
- Arrange pepper rings, mushrooms and olives over cheese.
- Sprinkle with Parmesan cheese.
- Broil 5″ from heat until cheeses are melted.
- Gently slide to serving platter; cut into 8 wedges.
- Serves 4.

PRAIRIE MORNING

Northeastern Colorado is fittingly called the Golden Plains. Expansive reaches of golden wheat and grassland cover the gracefully flowing terrain that once was black with buffalo. A fresh pink and gold sunrise marks a prairie morning. A prairie dog arises from his burrow like a sentinel surveying his charge. The gentle songs of prairie birds and the sweet smell of buffalo grass provide the background. The panorama is dotted with cheerful blotches of color from literally scores of native wildflowers. Throughout the vast area tepee rings of stone and battle sites mark the red man's struggle to hold this boundless land, whose grass he called the carpet of the Great Spirit.

Garden Burgers

1 lb Coleman Natural Beef Ground Chuck or Natural Ground Round

1 egg

¼ cup grated carrot

¼ cup grated zucchini

¼ cup chopped green peppers

2 tbsp finely chopped celery

2 tsp chopped onion

4-6 Schmidt's Bakery Hamburger Buns

4-6 lettuce leaves

4-6 tomato slices

pickle slices

ketchup, mustard or mayonnaise

- Mix together meat and egg.
- Add carrots, zucchini, green peppers, celery and onion.
- Mix thoroughly and form into 4-6 patties; broil 4-6 minutes per side until desired doneness.
- Place in buns along with lettuce, tomato, pickles and ketchup, mustard or mayonnaise.
- Serves 4-6.

Mapo Tofu

2 tbsp vegetable oil

24 oz White Wave Tofu, drained and cut into 1" cubes

¼ cup vegetable oil

2 cups thinly sliced Inch By Inch Onions

1 large bunch Piedmont Farms Broccoli, cut into 3" spears

2 cups sliced mushrooms

2 cups soaked, sliced Shiitake mushrooms

2 tbsp cornstarch

2 tbsp cold water

2 cups cooked rice

walnuts and chopped green onion to garnish

Sauce:

¼ cup soy sauce

¼ cup dry sherry

1 tbsp toasted sesame oil

1½ tbsp grated fresh ginger

3 tbsp tomato sauce

1 cup water

3 cloves garlic, pressed

2 tbsp vinegar

cayenne

- Sauté tofu in 2 tbsp oil until light skin forms on tofu, 5-10 minutes; set aside.
- Whisk all sauce ingredients together and set aside.
- Heat ¼ cup oil in wok to medium high heat.
- Sauté onions until soft, add broccoli and sauté additional 3-4 minutes.
- Add mushrooms; sauté for 3 minutes, stirring often.
- Pour in sauce and add tofu.
- Lower heat; cover, simmer until all ingredients are hot.
- Dissolve cornstarch in water; add to wok.
- Simmer until sauce thickens.
- Serve on rice, garnished with walnuts and chopped green onions.
- Serves 4-5.

HISTORIC FARMERS

According to writers of Colorado agricultural history, the most important historic group of farmers in Colorado belonged to the Union Colony, which established the town of Greeley. Today, Greeley is the county seat of Weld County in northern Colorado, one of the nation's richest agricultural counties. Nathan C. Meeker devised the plan for the colony while he was serving as agricultural editor for Horace Greeley's New York *Tribune*. His plan allowed for joining the group with a $5 membership fee and a $150 payment. Members could then settle on twelve thousand acres purchased from an agency of the Denver Pacific Railroad. He attracted 442 members and the colony began in 1870.

Black Bean Chili Pie

½ (11 oz) pkg Mitie Mixes Black Beans
8 cups water
½ lb ground beef, browned
2 tsp chili powder
½ tsp cumin
1 (4 oz) can diced green chilies, drained
½ cup sliced black olives
¼ cup chopped green onions
1 cup crushed El Dorado Tortilla Chips
½ cup plain yogurt
½ cup shredded Monterey Jack cheese
½ cup shredded Cheddar cheese
¼ cup sliced black olives
1 (2.5 oz) jar sliced mushrooms, drained
½ cup crushed El Dorado Tortilla Chips

- Cook black beans in water 1½ hours or until tender; drain.
- Combine beans with ground beef, chili powder, cumin, green chilies, black olives and green onions.
- Cover bottom of 9″ glass pie pan with 1 cup crushed tortilla chips.
- Spread bean mixture over chips; cover with yogurt.
- Top with Monterey Jack cheese, Cheddar cheese, black olives, mushrooms and crushed tortilla chips. Cover with foil.
- Bake in 375 degree oven 15 minutes.
- Uncover, bake 20 minutes more until heated thoroughly.
- Serve with lettuce and tomatoes.
- Serves 6.

Grilled Reuben On Rye

butter

8 slices Schmidt's Dark Rye Bread

1 lb cooked Custom Corned Beef, thinly sliced

1 (8 oz) can sauerkraut, drained

4 thick slices Bar-S Swiss Cheese

mayonnaise or thousand island dressing

- Lightly butter 1 side of 4 slices of rye bread; place on heated grill or skillet.
- Add 4 oz corned beef, ¼ cup sauerkraut and 1 slice cheese to each.
- Spread dressing on remaining 4 slices of bread to complete the sandwiches.
- Grill until cheese starts to melt; turn and grill other side.
- Makes 4 sandwiches.

Tofu Enchiladas

Sauce:

8-10 La Tolteca Tortillas

oil for cooking

1 (15 oz) can tomato sauce

1½ tsp garlic powder

1 medium onion, chopped

¼ cup diced green chilies

4 tsp chili powder

¼ tsp oregano

¼ tsp basil

Filling:

16 oz White Wave Tofu, drained and crumbled

½ cup grated White Wave Cheddar Style Soy A Melt

½ cup grated White Wave Mozzarella Style Soy A Melt

Topping:

½ cup grated White Wave Mozzarella Style Soy A Melt

½ cup sliced olives

- Heat tortillas individually in frying pan with ⅛″ hot oil until soft.
- Preheat oven to 350 degrees.
- Mix sauce ingredients together in saucepan; simmer 15 minutes.
- Mix all filling ingredients together.
- Place 2-3 tbsp filling in each tortilla; roll tightly and place in baking dish seam down.
- Cover tortillas with sauce and sprinkle with soy mozzarella and olives.
- Bake, covered, 15-20 minutes at 350 degrees.
- Serves 4-6.

SILVERHEEL'S STORY

At the very beginnings of the South Platte River sat Buckskin Joe, a town named for the leather clothing which a prominent citizen of the town—Joe Higgenbottom—wore. A nearby mountain was named Silverheels, for a beautiful dance hall girl who hailed from Buckskin Joe. She was affectionately given the nickname Silverheels when a miner made her a pair of shoes with silver heels. A smallpox epidemic hit the town and Silverheels was tending the miners and comforting the dying. Of course, she caught the disease as well and disappeared. A few years later a heavily veiled woman was seen walking, spirit like, through the town. It was Silverheels, whose beauty had been destroyed by the disease, thus the reason for the veil. True story or not? Who can tell? Nevertheless, Silverheels Mountain remains.

Black Bean Tortilla Bake

1 (11 oz) pkg Mitie Mixes Black Beans

8 cups water

½ lb ground beef

½ cup chopped onion

1 (16 oz) can Mile High Stewed Tomatoes

½ cup enchilada sauce

1 tsp Colorado Spice Co. Chili Powder

1 tsp cumin

¼ tsp pepper

6 La Tolteca Tortillas

1 (3 oz) pkg cream cheese, softened

1 (4 oz) can diced green chilies, drained

½ cup shredded Monterey Jack cheese

- Put black beans in water. Bring to boil, reduce heat, simmer 1½ hours, or until tender.
- In large skillet, brown ground beef and onion; drain off fat.
- Stir in beans, stewed tomatoes, enchilada sauce, chili powder, cumin and pepper; bring to boil, cover and simmer 5 minutes.
- Pour half of sauce into 12″ x 7½″ x 2″ glass baking dish.
- Spread tortillas with cream cheese; top with green chilies. Fold in half and arrange over sauce.
- Pour remaining sauce down the center. Cover and bake in 350 degree oven 15 minutes.
- Uncover; sprinkle cheese over top. Bake 5 minutes more or until bubbly.
- Serves 3-6.

Bagels Benedict

2 Agnes' Very Very Take & Bake Bagels

4 thin slices Bar-S Ham or
Canadian Bacon

butter

water

4 eggs

Hollandaise Sauce:

3 eggs, separated

3 tbsp boiling water

1½ tbsp lemon juice or tarragon
vinegar, warmed

½ cup melted Rocky Mountain Butter

¼ tsp salt

⅛ tsp cayenne

- To make hollandaise, beat egg yolks, in top of double boiler with wire whisk, until thickened.
- Add 1 tbsp water; beat again until eggs thicken. Repeat until 3 tbsp have been used.
- Beat in lemon juice or tarragon vinegar.
- Remove from heat; whisk in melted butter.
- Add salt and cayenne; whisk until thick. Set aside.
- Prepare bagels according to pkg directions.
- Fry ham or Canadian bacon in small amount of butter to desired doneness.
- Remove from pan onto paper towel; set aside.
- Fill frying pan with 1½″ of water; heat to boiling.
- Reduce to simmer; gently break egg into water.
- Cook to desired doneness, 3-5 minutes.
- Slice bagels in half; place 1 slice of meat on each half.
- Top with poached eggs and desired amount of hollandaise sauce.
- Serves 4.

A BOUNTY OF CROPS

Farming and ranching in Colorado is a fascinating blend of products. Beef cattle and calves is the largest category, totaling almost sixty-four percent, and when combined with hogs, sheep and lambs, poultry, dairy products and other animals, this segment makes up nearly seventy-two percent of total cash receipts. But other crops, although smaller in revenues, still have an important place. Wheat is a major food grain raised here, potatoes, corn, onions, beans, hay, apples, peaches, honey, carnations, roses and many other crops contribute to this all-important sector of Colorado's economy.

Liver Sauté with Cauliflower Au Gratin

8 small slices Coleman Calves Liver
1 (12 oz) can Budweiser® Beer, divided
salt, pepper and garlic powder
2 (10 oz) pkgs cauliflower au gratin
¼ cup Robinson Butter

- Preheat oven to 400 degrees.
- Place liver slices in shallow dish.
- Cover slices with 1¼ cups beer; let stand at room temperature 1 hour; drain.
- Sprinkle liver slices with salt, pepper and garlic powder to taste; set aside.
- Place cauliflower in shallow casserole and spoon 1¼ cups beer on top.
- Bake in oven 30-35 minutes, or until bubbly.
- When cauliflower is ready, heat butter in skillet.
- Add liver slices and brown quickly on both sides.
- Serve liver with cauliflower au gratin.
- Serves 4.

Suzanne's Stroganoff

¾ lb chopped mushrooms

1 cup chopped onions

3 tbsp Meadow Gold Butter

4 cups Meadow Gold Sour Cream

3 tbsp Marsala wine

1 tbsp F & J Worcestershire Sauce

½ tsp salt

¼ tsp dillweed

6-8 sticks Earth Dance Vegetarian Jerki, broken into ½" squares

6 cups chopped broccoli

4 cups Salvatore's Wide Egg Noodles

green onions or parsley to garnish

- Sauté first 3 ingredients until onions are soft. Combine with next 5 ingredients and cook at low heat 30 minutes.
- Remove from heat and add jerki.
- While sauce is cooking, steam broccoli; cook egg noodles according to pkg directions; drain.
- Spread noodles on plate, cover with broccoli, then cover with sauce.
- Garnish with green onions or parsley.
- Serves 6.

Apple-Shrimp Sauté

¼ cup unsweetened pineapple juice

1 tbsp soy sauce

⅛ tsp All American Seasonings Ginger

½ lb Keeton Fisheries Shrimp, cleaned and deveined

1 Colorado Golden Delicious Apple, cored and sliced

½ cup fresh or frozen peas

1 stalk celery, sliced diagonally

1 green onion, diagonally sliced

1 tbsp cold water

1 tsp cornstarch

- Combine pineapple juice, soy sauce and ginger; bring to boil.
- Add shrimp, apple, peas, celery and green onion.
- Simmer, stirring frequently, 5 minutes or until thoroughly heated and shrimp is cooked.
- Combine water and cornstarch; blend into hot juices in pan.
- Cook and stir until thickened and clear.
- Serves 2.

Sailing on Lake Dillon

Photo by Anne Krause

FIRE FIGHTER GAMES

One of the forms of recreation that developed within the communities which sprung up around the mines was the competition between the towns' volunteer fire departments. Two kinds of races were held—Hook and Ladder and Hose. The Hook and Ladder companies raced 200 feet and put a man atop a thirty-foot ladder. Hose companies had to run 500 feet to a hydrant, lay 200 feet of hose and get water through the nozzle. There was also head to head competition to simply see whose company was the fastest. In those days men, not horses, pulled the fire engines. Wagering was extensive, and it is reported that at the Colorado state tournament of 1878 $150,000 was bet. One wonders though, who was at home protecting against fires during these competitions? Maybe that's why so many mining communities suffered devastating fires.

Easy Paella

1 (5.5 oz) pkg Spanish rice mix
1 cup Budweiser® Beer
1¼ cups water
1 tbsp butter
1 (5 oz) can boned chicken
1 (7.5 oz) can minced clams
1 (4 oz) can sliced mushrooms
1 cup frozen peas
¼ cup diced pimento
1 (10 oz) pkg frozen raw shrimp

- Cook Spanish rice according to pkg directions using beer, water and butter.

- When rice is almost tender, add flaked chicken, juice from clams and undrained mushrooms.

- Gently stir in frozen peas, pimento, clams and shrimp.

- Cover; simmer 15 minutes, or until peas and shrimp are cooked.

- If necessary, add more water to keep rice moist.

- Serve hot.

- Serves 4-6.

CLEANING UP THE GOLD MINERS

Idaho Springs was the site of one of the two initial discoveries of gold in Colorado in 1859. George Jackson, on his way to the high country to hunt, came across it while looking for water near his campsite. The rest is history. Many tales emerged from this community, but one in particular was endemic to the entire gold rush area. It seems that during the first year of gold mining the men had no means of washing body or clothes. Then, an enterprising man came along with huge iron kettles, wooden tubs and old fashioned lye soap, all for sale. Then a hardworking lady began the first laundry, and the effort to clean up the town had started. Those miners were pretty sturdy people come to think of it. Lye soap would clean anything, and take a few inches of skin with it.

Calico Casserole

1 (11 oz) pkg Mitie Mixes Calico Bean Soup Mix	• Soak soup mix according to pkg directions.
5 cups water	• Cover with 5 cups water.
3 slices Bar-S Bacon or ½ cup chopped Bar-S Ham	• Cook 2½ hours or until tender; 35 minutes in pressure cooker.
1 large onion, chopped	• Drain, reserving liquid.
⅓ cup brown sugar	• Place beans in greased 11¾" x 7½" baking dish.
½ tsp Colorado Spice Co. Dry Mustard	• Fry bacon or ham.
¼ cup vinegar	• Add onion; sauté.
¼ cup ketchup	• Add brown sugar, dry mustard, vinegar and ketchup. Cook 5 minutes. Pour over beans.
	• Add reserved liquid to barely cover beans.
	• Bake, uncovered, 1 hour at 350 degrees.
	• Add additional liquid, if needed.
	• Serves 8-10.

A PINCH OF GOLD

You might wonder how people paid for food, liquor, supplies and baths in such towns as Idaho Springs, on the edge of civilization. Currency and coin were in short supply, so gold dust was the medium of exchange. But how to measure that in order to be properly paid? Primarily, it consisted of the buyer taking a pinch of gold dust between thumb and forefinger and that was computed to be one dollar. However, a person with big fingers could outdo a person with little ones. You can imagine the arguments and gunfights which must have occurred over such transactions. When the scales for weighing the gold finally arrived in the area, a lot of problems were solved.

Chorizo Burrito

½ onion, diced

1 tbsp vegetable oil

1 lb Old West Smoked Chorizo, sliced into bite-size pieces

2-3 San Luis Valley Potatoes

salt and pepper

6 eggs

2 tbsp water

Mexican Bear Flour Tortillas

1 cup President's Pride Cheddar Cheese

green chilies or salsa (optional)

- In skillet, sauté onion in oil until translucent.
- Add chorizo pieces, potatoes, salt and pepper; sauté until heated.
- Whip eggs and water in bowl until light and fluffy; add to mixture in skillet and stir until desired consistency.
- Steam tortillas until softened by placing them over a pot of boiling water.
- Meanwhile, fill each tortilla with egg mixture and fold over, making a pocket.
- Sprinkle with shredded Cheddar cheese and smother with green chilies or salsa.
- Serve immediately.
- Serves 6-8.

MEATS & FISH

The Broadmoor, Colorado Springs

Photo by Jeff Andrew

CAMERAS CLICK ON HIGHWAY 82

On leaving Glenwood Springs for Aspen, along Colorado Highway 82, visitors find an area which is probably photographed more than any other in the state. Near Maroon Creek are the world-famous Maroon Bells— two giant, snow-capped peaks. A mountain lake lies at their feet. It's a picture perfect setting, and the area contains numerous hiking trails for studying and photographing the native trees, grasses and wildflowers. When visited in the fall, as the aspen trees turn to gold, the setting is almost too lovely for words—or pictures. And while you are in this area, a stop in Snowmass is more than warranted, particularly to visit the largest full time working dog sled kennel in the world—the Krabloonik Kennels. Finish off your visit with an outstanding game meal at the Krabloonik Restaurant situated in a rustic log cabin.

Grilled Colorado Bass

4 Aquafarm Associates Colorado Mountain Bass
lemon wedges to garnish

Marinade:
½ cup Pikes Peak Vineyards White Wine
1 cup soy sauce
3 tbsp High Country Honey
½ cup vegetable oil
1 tsp grated ginger

- Combine all marinade ingredients.
- Pour over bass and set in refrigerator to marinade 1-2 hours.
- Remove; grill over medium coals 3-5 minutes per side.
- Baste with marinade while grilling.
- Garnish with lemon wedges.
- Serves 4.

Fried Shrimp in Beer Batter

1 lb Keeton Fisheries Shrimp, peeled
Larry's Seafood Seasoning
1 cup half and half
1 cup Mt. Mama Unbleached
All-Purpose Flour
½ cup cornstarch
3 tsp baking powder, divided
1 egg, beaten
½ can Michelob® Beer
vegetable oil

- Rinse shrimp in cold water and pat dry.
- Lightly season shrimp with seafood seasoning.
- Place shrimp in bowl and cover with cream. Allow to soak for 30 minutes.
- Mix the flour, cornstarch, baking powder and 1 tbsp of seafood seasoning.
- Mix egg with beer; add cream from the shrimp.
- Add 1 tbsp oil to the flour mixture; knead until uniform mixture is achieved.
- Slowly add the beer mixture to the flour mixture. Whip into a smooth batter.
- Drop shrimp into the batter; roll to coat.
- Remove shrimp 1 at a time and drop into hot oil, working quickly.
- Allow shrimp to cook to a golden brown, then remove from the oil.
- Cook in 2-3 batches to prevent crowding in the cooking oil.
- Serves 3-4.

EARLY FARMERS

The origins of agriculture in Colorado go back many centuries, to when the Anasazi Indians tried their hand at corn, squash and beans. Later, the settlers at Bent's Fort did the same with mixed success. There were even some early efforts in the San Luis Valley by people from old and New Mexico. It was not until several years later that progress really began. That was when the mines opened and the demand for food grew dramatically. Emigrants from the East, California and Texas moved in and began dealing with Colorado weather, water and soil, to raise crops.

Oven Broiled Alaskan Halibut

1 cup olive oil
1 tbsp All American Seasonings Oregano
1 crushed All American Seasonings Bay Leaf
1 lemon, juiced
2 garlic cloves, crushed
2 tbsp All American Seasonings Basil
1 tsp celery salt
1 tsp freshly cracked black pepper
6 halibut steaks, 1" thick
1 (15 oz) can Dowling's Mussels Sailor Style Soup

- Combine all ingredients, except fish and soup in a bowl; mix thoroughly.
- Add fish to marinade; refrigerate 2-3 hours.
- Turn 1-2 times to make sure steaks are well coated.
- Remove steaks from marinade; let drain for a few minutes.
- Place on well greased pan or foil and broil.
- Baste the fish several times as it cooks.
- For the sauce, heat soup in saucepan; season to taste.
- Place cooked steaks on heated platter and top with sauce.
- Serve immediately.
- Serves 6.

THEN CAME THE LOGGERS

One of the side industries which rapidly developed during the mining era was logging. The miners needed lumber for sluice boxes and particularly to shore up their diggings the deeper they went into a mountain. In Clear Creek County, site of the Idaho Springs find, logging soon became the second biggest industry, next to mining. The demand for lumber was extensive, not only for the mines, but for people to build homes and businesses. Huge steam engines were hauled in to run the sawmills, aiding production greatly. By the end of the 19th century the areas closest to the various mining settlements had been almost completely cut of available lumber. This forced loggers and mill hands to move up near the timberline for supplies. By the 1940s logging ended, the result of the mines closing down.

Southern Fried Catfish

2-4 lbs Keeton Fisheries Catfish
Larry's Seafood Seasoning
⅛ tsp garlic powder
2 cups Hungarian® All-Purpose Flour
2 cups white corn meal
peanut oil

- Rinse fish and lightly season with seafood seasoning and garlic powder.
- Mix flour and corn meal; put in large plastic bag.
- Add fish to bag; shake gently.
- Heat oil in qt pot.
- Remove fish from bag carefully; gently drop into hot oil.
- Fry fish until golden brown, remove and serve at once.
- Serves 4.

POPULAR PIKES PEAK

Lt. Zebulon Montgomery Pike first mentioned the mountain which now bears his name, Pikes Peak, in his journal of November 15, 1806. Fortunately for us, but unfortunately for Lt. Pike, he was actually slightly lost as he was looking for the headwaters of the Red River. However, thanks to the good Lieutenant we all now have Pikes Peak to visit. The pinnacle of Pikes Peak has been reached by more people than any other mountain in the world except Mount Fujiyama in Japan. They have traveled by foot, burro, carriage, cog train and automobile to make the ascent.

Baked Trout

2 whole Four Seasons Trout, cleaned and dressed
2 cups dry sherry
½ cup F & J Worcestershire Sauce
dash F & J Piqueosot Sauce
1 tsp salt
½ tsp black pepper
3 tbsp melted Graves Dairy Butter
cooked rice

- Preheat oven to 350 degrees.
- Place trout in shallow glass pan.
- Combine sherry, Worcestershire sauce, piqueosot sauce, salt and pepper. Pour over trout.
- Cover; refrigerate 4-5 hours.
- Place trout in shallow baking pan; spoon on marinade. Bake 20 minutes.
- Remove from oven; baste with butter.
- Return to oven to bake 10 minutes more.
- Serve with rice.
- Serves 2.

THE MONUMENT

Water inexorably shaped the over 20,000 acres comprising the Colorado National Monument, and water determines what lives here. Streams have meandered throughout the area, cutting the bedrock and leaving cottonwoods and willows in their wake. Otherwise it is sage brush, saltbush, serviceberry and whatever else can survive in the dramatically changing conditions.

What has man done in this place? In most cases simply driven the twenty-three mile Rimrock Drive to observe whatever he can about the Monument. The Drive is a story unto itself. It was hewn from the sandstone walls of the Monument by Civilian Conservation Corps workers in the 1930s. The work was exceptionally hard, and could be dangerous, as witness the death of nine workers in a blasting accident during the construction. But with pick and shovel these workers made it possible for those of us today to view the Monument in all its glory.

Creamy Dilled Salmon

1 cup Mountain High® Plain Yoghurt, divided

3 tbsp water

1 tbsp vegetable oil

½ tsp dillweed, divided

4 salmon steaks, 1" thick

2 tbsp Meadow Gold Butter

1 egg, slightly beaten

- In 12" x 7" baking dish, combine ½ cup yoghurt, water, oil and ¼ tsp dillweed.
- Add salmon; cover and refrigerate 1 hour.
- Remove salmon from sauce; grill or broil until fish flakes with a fork.
- Meanwhile, in small saucepan, melt butter; stir in remaining yoghurt, dillweed and egg. Over low heat, cook and stir until thickened, being careful not to boil.
- Serve warm with salmon.
- Serves 4.

CENTRAL CITY

In Colorado, when one mentions Central City, the phrase "once the richest square mile on earth" jumps to mind, for Central City was one of the first two discoveries, in 1859, which fueled the state's gold rush.

The Central City area produced more than $125 million in precious metals, while Gilpin County, its home, produced nearly a half-billion dollars. Central City was not only Colorado's first major boom city, it was, and always will, be the state's most typical mining community.

During the town's heyday, the The Teller House Hotel was home for many of the rich and famous. Not only did the Bonanza King, Horace Tabor, visit, but so did the poet Walt Whitman, explorer Henry M. Stanley, Mark Twain and President Ulysses S. Grant.

Of the latter's visit many tales abound, such as paving the Teller House walk with $12,000 worth of silver bricks for him to trod on as he stepped from his stagecoach upon arrival.

Batter Fried Fish with Orange Delight Sauce

1 cup Graves Dairy Milk
2 eggs, well beaten
1½ cup Wheat Land Farms Unbleached Flour
1 tsp baking powder
1 tsp salt
peanut oil for frying
2 lbs Aquafarm Associates Fish

Orange Delight Sauce:
3 tbsp More Than Mustard Country Style Mustard
6 tbsp orange marmalade

- Combine milk and eggs.
- Add milk mixture to flour, baking powder and salt; mix well.
- Heat oil.
- Dip fish in batter; then fry until golden brown.
- To make sauce, mix mustard and marmalade together well and serve with fish.
- Serves 4.

THE DEEPEST CANYON

Moving south from Montrose County, Colorado, one can experience the awesome Black Canyon of the Gunnison National Monument. One of the deepest and narrowest gorges in the world, its views are breathtaking. The canyon has been carved by the Gunnison River as it hurries to join the Colorado. Canyon walls tower as much as 3,000 feet above the rolling river. At "The Narrows," the rims of the canyon are only 1,300 feet apart. As the sun shines almost every day, the deep and narrow canyon walls are shrouded in shadows, hence the name "Black Canyon." To the east is Blue Mesa Reservoir, the largest body of water in the state—8,000 acres!

Mushroom Turkey Piquant

2 tbsp Graves Dairy Butter, divided
2 tbsp vegetable oil, divided
1 lb Rakhra Mushrooms, sliced
4 (3 oz) slices Barber's Turkey Breast, pounded to ¼"thickness
all-purpose flour
¼ cup dry sherry
1 (14.5 oz) can chicken broth
½ cup lemon juice
¼ cup water
¼ cup drained capers
salt and pepper
watercress and lemon slices to garnish

- In broad skillet, heat 1 tbsp each butter and oil to sizzling.
- Add mushrooms; sauté over medium heat until tender but still firm. Remove to warm platter; set aside.
- Dust turkey slices generously with flour.
- Sauté in remaining butter and oil 3-5 minutes, turning once when edges of turkey become opaque.
- Remove turkey to platter with mushrooms.
- Stir in additional tsp of flour into skillet.
- Stir in sherry, then broth, lemon juice and water. Simmer 5 minutes.
- Stir in mushrooms, turkey and capers. Season with salt and pepper. Simmer to heat thoroughly.
- Garnish with watercress and lemon slices.
- Serves 4.

CENTRAL CITY'S OPERA HOUSE

The Opera House in Central City has seen many an interesting performance. From rough miners to established stars, it has been home to enjoyable performances for nearly as long as Central City has existed. In particular, since the early 1930s the Opera House has been the site of both plays and operas, especially during a multi-week period each summer. Opera has taken the focus during recent times including regular performances of "The Ballad of Baby Doe," especially popular in Central City since that is where the legendary lady really received her start. However, the first performance after the refurbishment in 1932, was "Camille" with Lillian Gish.

Despite the changes of our modern era, Central City has attempted to retain the old flavor whenever possible. The town displays life as it was lived in the 1870s in a cultured community.

Beer-Broiled Shrimp

¾ cup Coors Beer
3 tbsp vegetable oil
2 tbsp snipped parsley
4 tsp Worcestershire sauce
1 clove garlic, minced
½ tsp salt
⅛ tsp pepper
2 lbs large shrimp, unshelled

- Combine all ingredients, except shrimp.
- Add shrimp; stir. Cover; let stand at room temperature 1 hour.
- Drain, reserving marinade.
- Place shrimp on well greased broiler rack; broil 4"-5" from heat 4 minutes.
- Turn, brush with marinade. Broil 2-4 minutes more, or until bright pink.
- Serves 6.
©Meredith Corporation 1981.

PROGRESSIVE FARMERS

The Union Colony colonists, emigrants from the East, are said to have been unusually intelligent, temperate and well informed. They led many technological advances that paved the way for the significance of this vast agricultural area today. They popularized the use of alfalfa as a substitute for wild grass, imported honey bees for pollination, and established potatoes as Colorado's first cash crop. The alfalfa nourished the soil with nitrogen, increasing the potato yield to a profitable level. They found markets for their potatoes in Texas and Oklahoma, which lasted from 1886 to 1910. A blight ruined the crop over the next several years, declining its importance to the colony's economy. In the meanwhile, the colonists used their collective resources to establish advanced mechanical technology, reapers, harvesters, combines, fencing and irrigation canals for the area.

Pan-Fried Whole Trout or Filets

2-3 lbs Cline Colorado Trout
2 tsp salt
¼ tsp ground pepper
½ cup Horizon Yellow Corn Meal
½ cup Hungarian® All-Purpose Flour
6 tbsp vegetable oil
1 lemon, cut into wedges

- Wash trout under cold running water; pat dry with paper towels. Sprinkle with salt and pepper.
- Mix corn meal and flour.
- In heavy skillet, heat oil over moderate heat.
- Roll trout in corn meal mixture; shake off excess and put in skillet.
- Fry 4-5 minutes on each side, until golden brown and flaky.
- Serve with lemon wedges.
- Serves 4.

TWO BOOMS FOR LEADVILLE

Today a town of a few thousand people on the road to Independence Pass and entry to Aspen, the Leadville of the late 1800's was filled with 30,000 or more people seeking their fortunes. Many found what they were looking for or died in the attempt.

Although it started with a gold strike the story of Leadville truly turns on the discovery of silver. Gold miners had noted the heavy black sand which clogged their sluice boxes, and cussed it. But it was later found to contain rich deposits of silver and the second boom began. We can thank Uncle Billy Stevens and A.B. Wood for having the sand analyzed and discovering the rich silver content.

The story of Leadville is much like the story of Colorado . . . boom and bust. During its peak it was considered one of the wealthiest and roughest towns in the world. Today, it is much more sedate, but the hills surrounding this community have tales to tell of its historical significance to the state and the Nation.

Swordfish With Mustard and Hazelnuts

1½ lbs swordfish	• Brush fish with mustard and coat in hazelnuts.
5 tbsp More Than Mustard Country Style Mustard	
1 cup toasted, hulled and finely ground hazelnuts	• Add oil to pan and heat.
	• Add fish and sauté 3 minutes on each side.
4 tbsp safflower oil	• Squeeze fresh lemon juice on top and serve.
1 lemon, juiced	
	• Serves 3-4.

THE FIRST "BONANZA KING"

The tale of Leadville is really the story of Horace Tabor, the first of the "Bonanza Kings." A Vermont stone-cutter, he and his wife Augusta established a general store, bar, post office and hotel to serve prospectors in the Leadville area. He had been unsuccessful in his own mining attempts, while he watched his customers become wealthy. One day in 1878 two broke, but ambitious, wanderers came into Horace's store and asked for a grubstake. At first Tabor turned them down, but when they returned again he let them have $17.00 worth of supplies, and off they went.

Upon stopping to rest while climbing a nearby hill they decided to begin digging right where they were. Down only a few feet they struck ore, one of the richest veins of silver found to that point. Because of his grubstake, Tabor received one-third of the mine which produced $80,000 or more per month. Tabor was on his way to becoming one of the state's best known and wealthiest characters.

Oriental Lamb Chops

3 tbsp dark Oriental sesame oil

4 (5 oz) Cedaredge Boneless Double Loin Lamb Chops

1 medium yellow onion, finely chopped

2 cloves garlic, peeled and minced

3 tbsp soy sauce

3 tbsp Oriental chili paste

1 cup orange marmalade

1½ tbsp rice wine vinegar

1 tbsp minced fresh gingerroot

- Heat oil in large skillet.
- Add lamb chops and brown lightly on both sides. Remove from pan.
- Add the onion and garlic to the oil; cook 20 minutes, or until tender.
- Add soy sauce, chili paste, marmalade, rice vinegar and gingerroot. Simmer 2 minutes, stirring constantly.
- Return lamb chops to skillet. Cover and cook over low heat 7 minutes, turning the chops once, halfway through.
- Serve immediately, spooning sauce over chops.
- Serves 4.

HORACE AND BABY DOE

Despite Horace Tabor's success in silver, he died penniless. The drop in silver prices during the 1890s and the scandal surrounding his romance with the now famous Baby Doe, whom he later married after divorcing his first wife, Augusta, are blamed. Elizabeth McCourt Tabor had been named Baby Doe by the miners of Central City during her stay there. Tabor's open relationship with her was widely known and turned into a scandal before it was finally settled.

Tabor was the richest man in the state and lived like it. For some time he kept Baby Doe comfortably ensconced in fancy hotels, before eventually going through with his divorce and marrying her. But despite his wealth and investments, when the price of silver dropped dramatically his wealth followed that drop. He died a bitter man in 1899, and Baby Doe went back to Leadville to live out her life in poverty.

Breaded Lamb Chops

1 cup crushed buttery crackers
1 tbsp grated Parmesan cheese
½ tsp crushed, dried rosemary leaves
⅛ tsp black pepper
8 Colorado Lamb Loin or Rib Chops, 1" thick, trimmed
1 egg, beaten
2 tbsp Rocky Mountain Butter

- Combine cracker crumbs, cheese, rosemary and pepper.
- Coat both sides of lamb chops with egg, then dip in crumb mixture.
- In large frying pan, melt butter over medium heat; add chops. Cook over medium heat 5-7 minutes, or until browned on both sides.
- Place on rack in shallow pan. Bake at 325 degrees 20-25 minutes, or until desired doneness.
- Serves 4.

"THE BALLAD OF BABY DOE"

Purportedly, Horace Tabor's last words to Baby Doe were "hang onto the Matchless (Mine)." Tabor believed it might once again rise to its former greatness. Baby Doe followed her husband's advice and held on to the mine until her death. The Matchless Cabin, where Baby Doe lived and died, is now open to the public visiting Leadville and tells its story through words and pictures. The story of these two is recalled in an opera entitled, "The Ballad of Baby Doe," which is performed regularly in the world-famous opera house in Central City, Colorado.

Other Leadville sites that will help tell you its story are the Tabor Opera House, Vendome Hotel, Augusta Tabor Cottage and a molybdenum mine producing over half of the free world's molybdenum.

Rocky Mountain Red Roast

salt

pepper

all-purpose flour

4 lbs Colorado Beef Roast, any cut

3 tbsp vegetable oil

1 (8 oz) can tomato sauce

1 cup water

1½ cups Rocky Mountain Red Wine

½ tsp oregano

½ tsp rosemary

1 (4 oz) can mushroom pieces

2 medium San Luis Valley Potatoes, halved lengthwise

2 carrots, halved lengthwise

1 medium onion, quartered

- Salt, pepper and flour roast on all sides.
- Brown quickly in oil, in a heavy, deep-sided skillet.
- Add tomato sauce, water, wine and herbs. Cover and simmer over low heat for 1½-2 hours.
- Turn roast over occasionally, spooning the gravy over the meat.
- Add vegetables 1 hour before serving; re-cover and continue to simmer until all is tender.
- Serves 6-8.

HOUSE RULES

Hotels, we have all loved them, hated them and most surely left them. No different in Colorado, although sometimes the rules of the house do change. Here are the rules of one such establishment provided to us by author Sandra Dallas:

1. Don't shoot the pianist, he's doing his damndest.
2. Don't swear, damn you.
3. Beds, 50 cents; with sheets, 75 cents.
4. No horses above the first floor.
5. No more than five in a bed.
6. Warmth provided by horse blankets, liquor and Christian zeal.
7. Funerals on the house.

Maybe you had better check the rules closely the next time you stop for the night!

Lamb Chops A La Orange

3 tbsp vegetable oil

6 Colorado Loin Lamb Chops, ½" thick, trimmed

½ cup Marquest Orange Juice

¼ cup soy sauce

1½ tsp fresh ginger

½ tsp salt

2 cloves garlic, minced

¼ tsp pepper

½ tsp sugar

2 small oranges, peeled and sectioned

- Heat oil in skillet.
- Lightly brown chops in oil. Drain on paper towels.
- Place browned chops in a shallow baking dish that can be covered.
- Combine orange juice, soy sauce, ginger, salt, garlic, pepper and sugar; pour over chops.
- Cover and refrigerate 2 hours, turning once.
- Remove from refrigerator; leave cover on. Bake at 350 degrees, 45-55 minutes, or until chops are tender.
- Place orange sections on chops. Replace cover; bake 10 minutes.
- Spoon sauce over chops before serving.
- Serves 6.

Buffalo Chuck Roast

1 (2-4 lb) Lay Valley Bison Ranch
Buffalo Chuck Roast

½ cup water

1 pkg dry onion soup

¼ cup Eartharvest Unbleached
All-Purpose Flour

1 cup Meadow Gold Sour Cream

1 (4.5 oz) can mushrooms

salt and pepper

- In slow cooker, place roast, water and onion soup. Cook on low setting 6-8 hours.

- Remove roast; let stand 15 minutes.

- To juices add flour, sour cream and mushrooms. Stir to make gravy. Season with salt and pepper to taste.

- Thinly slice roast; top with gravy.

- Serves 8-10.

Colorado Lamb Chops and Peppers

4 Montfort Loin Lamb Chops, trimmed

4 tbsp vegetable oil

2 onions, thinly sliced

1 clove garlic, chopped

1 lb Golden West Tomatoes, peeled,
seeded and chopped

2 Golden West Green Bell Peppers,
seeded and cut in strips

1 Golden West Red Bell Pepper, seeded
and cut in strips

1 tsp crushed coriander seeds

salt and pepper

1 cup Pikes Peak Vineyards Colorado
White Wine

1 tbsp Cream of the Valley Tomato Paste

- Brown chops in oil in large skillet. Add onions and garlic, cover and cook 10 minutes until onions are translucent.

- Add tomatoes, peppers, coriander, salt and pepper. Cover and cook 15 minutes until chops are tender. Remove chops from pan and keep hot.

- Raise heat and add wine; cook uncovered until liquid is reduced by half, stirring.

- Add tomato paste; simmer 5 minutes. Spoon over chops and serve.

- Serves 4.

LAND OF ROCKS

Water and rock are the two things that stand out when viewing the Colorado National Monument near Grand Junction. The colors and views of this special place are spectacular and you can imagine early settlers or native Indians moving thru these mystical areas. The underlying rock to all of this is estimated to be two billion years old.

And what rock. Red rocks, slick rocks, sculptured rocks, enormous rocks, small rocks, every conceivable kind and shape and color. One cannot take in these vistas without considering what went into creating them and the sheer awesomeness of nature. Frigid in the winter, broiling in the summer, the rhythm of nature continually shapes this area and makes it new every time you see it.

Oven Cooked Bison Roast

1 (3-4 lb) Lay Valley Ranch Bison Roast
vegetable oil
garlic salt
seasoned salt
black pepper
Colorado Spice Co. Red Pepper
lemon juice
gravy

- Rub roast with oil, garlic salt, seasoned salt, black pepper and a small amount of red pepper. Lightly sprinkle roast with lemon juice.
- Wrap roast in aluminum foil.
- Seal foil around roast; place in roaster pan and bake at 300 degrees until a meat thermometer inserted in thickest portion registers 140 degrees.
- Remove roast immediately from oven when 140 degrees is reached; set aside for 15 minutes.
- Carve roast into thin slices and serve with gravy made from cooking juices, if desired.
- Serves 10-12.

TINY TOWN

Tiny Town! Sound interesting? Well this little town has been in existence for seventy-five years and is still drawing large crowds.

What exactly is Tiny Town? Best description would be a miniaturized town. Begun in 1915 as Turnerville, it opened in 1920 to the general public. The exhibits have varied over the years, but the miniature versions of homes, schools, churches, newspapers, barber shops and other buildings, have delighted children throughout the years. Besides the wonderful miniature buildings, Tiny Town has boasted an Indian display, pony rides and a puppet show over the years. But the attraction that has enchanted most visitors is the Tiny Town Railroad which makes regular runs around the entire display area.

Mushrooms and Rabbit Burgundy

¼ cup vegetable oil

4 lbs cooked, cubed Four Corners Rabbit

2 cloves garlic, minced

3 tbsp all-purpose flour

2 (10.5 oz) cans chicken broth

1½ cups Pikes Peak Vineyards Red Burgundy Wine

2 bay leaves

2 tsp salt

½ tsp thyme

¼ tsp pepper

4 cups sliced carrots

1 lb small white onions, quartered

2 lbs Rakhra Mushrooms, trimmed and sliced

cooked noodles

- In heavy saucepan heat oil; add rabbit, brown well on all sides.
- Sprinkle with garlic and flour. Stir to blend in flour; add broth, wine, bay leaves, salt, thyme and pepper.
- Add carrots, onions and mushrooms; bring to boil, reduce heat and simmer, covered, 1 hour.
- Serve over bed of noodles.
- Serves 6-8.

Durango and Silverton Narrow Gauge Train above the Animas River

Photo by Ron Ruhoff

GRAZING ON PRAIRIE GRASS

Prairie grass. It's native to Colorado and vital for sustenance of the state's cattle and buffalo. History tells us that in 1858, Jack Henderson turned his oxen loose after arriving in the Denver area from Kansas. He had no food for them and expected them to die during the harsh winter. But in the spring he found his oxen fat and healthy from a winter forage of prairie grass. The native grass did not break down in the frost like more moisture-laden Eastern grasses. Rather it stood tall, dried in the fall winds and retained its food value all winter.

Jicamese Beef

½ cup beef broth
¼ cup soy sauce
¼ cup sherry
1 tsp sesame oil
1 clove garlic, minced
1 tsp grated gingerroot
1 lb Colorado Beef Skirt Steak, cut into thin strips
1 cup jicama, peeled and cut into strips
1 cup Rosey Farms Red Pepper Strips
½ cup onion slices, cut in half
2 cups chopped Chinese cabbage
3 tbsp vegetable oil
½ tbsp cornstarch mixed with water
1 tbsp toasted sesame seeds
cooked rice
toasted sesame seeds

- Combine first 6 ingredients; mix well.
- Pour ¼ cup marinade on skirt steak; refrigerate 30 minutes. Reserve remaining marinade.
- Heat oil in heavy skillet or wok; add beef and stir-fry 3 minutes.
- Add vegetables and remaining marinade; stir.
- Cover and steam 3 minutes, or until vegetables are heated thoroughly but still crisp tender.
- Add cornstarch mixture, heating until bubbly.
- Serve over hot rice; sprinkle with toasted sesame seeds.
- Serves 4.

ENTERTAINING THE KIDS

For a few ideas on getting children's attention, consider:

Heritage Square in Golden, where a turn-of-the-century atmosphere exists. Plenty of shops to browse and gadgets to consider buying. The original wooden fort located there is now a trading post.

McGuckin Hardware and Sporting Goods in Boulder provides endless shelves filled with everything you will need for the home, or for camping or fishing—even furniture for the children.

Army Navy Surplus Stores in Denver, and in several other cities outside the state capital. There you will find tents for camping, canteens, camouflage goods, old uniforms and many other grand items for everyone in the family to rummage through.

Italian Meat Loaf

2 lbs. Coleman Natural Ground Chuck or Ground Round

1 (6 oz) can Cream of the Valley Tomato Paste

1 cup crushed saltine crackers

2 eggs

½ tsp salt

pinch of pepper

¼ cup finely chopped green pepper

½ cup finely chopped onion

1½ cups small curd cottage cheese

¼ tsp oregano

2 tsp chopped fresh parsley

½ cup sliced Rakhra Mushrooms

- Mix ground beef with tomato paste, ½ cup crushed crackers, eggs, salt, pepper, green pepper and onion.
- Put half the mixture into a 9" x 5" loaf pan.
- Mix cottage cheese with remaining crackers, oregano, parsley and mushrooms. Spread this mixture over first layer of meat in pan, then add the rest of the meat to form a loaf.
- Bake, uncovered, 1 hour at 350 degrees.
- Remove from oven. Let stand 5 minutes before serving.
- Serves 6.

WOOL VERSUS HIDE

Railroads were the key to development of agriculture in Colorado. Not only for the shipment of fed cattle back east, but to ship produce. Sheep and wool became major industries, and remain so today. But the beginnings were not easy. Sheep had been introduced from New Mexico to southern Colorado, disturbing the free-roaming cattlemen. Cattlemen didn't know yet that sheep could exist where cattle could not go. Thus, they felt the sheep herds were encroaching on their domain, and fought back. In one such incident, 16,000 sheep were killed near Pueblo. The Colorado government offered a $3,000 reward for those who committed the crime, but no one ever came forth with the information to claim the reward. As the range cattle industry died, the violence subsided and both industries began to grow side by side, fighting the elements rather than themselves.

Cola Brisket

1 (4-5 lb) Sisneros Brothers Beef Brisket

2 tbsp vegetable oil

1 cup chopped onions

1 cup chopped celery

salt and pepper

2 tsp Colorado Spice Co. Paprika, or to taste

2 cloves garlic, crushed

½ cup ketchup

¼ cup hot water

1 tbsp onion soup mix

1 (1.5 oz) pkg dry spaghetti sauce mix

1 cup Coca-Cola

- Place meat in large roasting pan and brush with oil on all sides.
- Sprinkle with onions and celery. Season to taste with salt, pepper and paprika. Place garlic on top.
- Mix ketchup with hot water, onion soup mix and dry spaghetti sauce mix, stirring to dissolve.
- Add cola.
- Pour mixture over meat; cover with foil.
- Bake at 350 degrees 2½-3 hours, basting every 20-30 minutes.
- Makes 6-8 servings.

TROUBLE AT ST. ELMO

Fire broke out in the St. Elmo post office in 1890, and the town's postmaster became the hero and the goat in a time of trouble. He saved the mail all right. But in doing so, he allowed a shipment of liquor to perish in the flames, and St. Elmo never forgave him.

Chicken and Grapes

1 cup finely crushed cracker crumbs

½ tsp salt

¼ tsp black pepper

¼ tsp basil leaves

¼ tsp tarragon

3 chicken breasts, split

¼ cup Meadow Gold Butter

¼ cup minced onion

¼ cup water

¾ cup Pikes Peak Vineyards Colorado White Wine

1 cube chicken bouillon

½ lb Rakhra Mushrooms, sliced

3 tbsp Meadow Gold Butter

2 cups Thompson seedless grapes

- Mix crumbs, salt, pepper, basil and tarragon.
- Remove skin from chicken breasts. Coat chicken in cracker crumbs.
- Heat ¼ cup butter in large skillet; brown chicken on all sides in butter.
- Place chicken in single layer in large baking pan.
- Add minced onion to butter in skillet; cook until soft. Pour in water and wine.
- Add bouillon cube. Bring liquid to boil, stirring to dissolve bouillon cube; pour around chicken.
- Bake, uncovered, in 375 degree oven 40 minutes.
- Meanwhile, sauté mushrooms in 3 tbsp butter. At end of 40 minutes baking time, add mushrooms and grapes to chicken. Continue to cook 8-10 minutes.
- Serves 6.

DOWN ON THE FARM

Agriculture is a nearly $4.0 billion industry in Colorado. Approximately 33.5 million acres are in farms and ranches throughout the state. The average size farm or ranch is 1,241 acres. When looking at what agriculture contributes to the state's economy there are three distinct segments: Agricultural production at the farm and ranch, which, according to the latest data consistent for all categories quoted, showed gross sales of $4.1 billion and contributed nearly 52,000 jobs; the food processing industry, which contributed $5.3 billion in sales and had nearly 26,000 jobs; and agricultural input, which are the sales and jobs that support the farm industry, that contributed $1.4 billion in sales and had 9,500 jobs in Colorado. Totals are $11.0 billion in sales and almost 87,000 jobs.

Beer-Grilled Chops

4 (1 lb) Sisneros Brothers Boneless Pork Loin Chops

Marinade:

¼ cup soy sauce

1 cup Michelob® Beer, at room temperature

2 tbsp brown sugar

2 tsp grated fresh gingerroot

- Mix marinade ingredients well.
- Place chops in plastic bag; pour in marinade, seal bag and refrigerate 4-24 hours.
- Prepare medium hot coals in grill.
- Remove chops from marinade; grill over medium hot coals 7-8 minutes per side, turning once.
- Serves 4.

COUNTRY TO THE NORTH

Just south of the small farming community of Wray, the site of the battle of Beecher Island, lies the peaceful shade of a cottonwood grove. A monument and gravestone tell the story. Nearby is a picnic ground for relaxing. Farther south lies Bonny Reservoir State Recreation Area. The 2,000 acre preserve is a high plains Garden of Eden, providing visitors a recreational lake with fourteen miles of shoreline and a living museum of wildlife, grasses and flowers native to the area.

Cattle ranches, fields of wheat, hay, sugar beets, corn and other grains, as well as oil and gas wells, are common in the soil-rich South Platte Valley. Busy farm towns, built near water supplies, provide services to the area's agricultural residents.

Julesburg, in the uppermost corner of the state, a stones throw from the Nebraska border, was the California Crossing of the Platte River on the Oregon Trail. The rich western lore of this one-time Pony Express station provides plenty of fuel for stories and yarns. Much of its history is relived in its museum.

Corned Beef Patties

3 cups cooked, chopped Russet Burbank Potatoes

2 cups chopped, cooked Temptee Brand Corned Beef

¼ cup grated onion

¼ cup Cream of the Valley Tomato Paste

½ tsp salt

½ tsp pepper

2 eggs, beaten

all-purpose flour

vegetable oil

- Combine first 7 ingredients; mix well.
- Shape into patties and chill thoroughly.
- Dredge patties in flour; fry in oil, browning on both sides.
- Serve immediately.
- Serves 8-10.

THE COLORADO MYSTIQUE

The weather in Colorado presents you with an exciting challenge each day. Yes, snow and ice and cold winds, but alternating with cobalt blue skies and a warming sun that melts the snow quickly in most areas. Some have said that there are only two seasons in the mountains, winter and the Fourth of July. But when you get up on a cloudless summer morning and watch what nature has wrought for you it is not hard to understand why weather helps make Colorado so attractive.

Peachy Smoked Pork Roast

½ tsp salt
½ tsp pepper
1 tsp ginger
2 tbsp vegetable oil
2 tbsp cider vinegar
½ cup brown sugar
3 tbsp F & J Piqueosot Chili Sauce
1 (29 oz) can peach slices in heavy syrup, undrained
1 (2 lb) Sisneros Brothers Boneless Pork Loin Roast
hickory chips

- In blender, combine salt, pepper, ginger, oil, vinegar, brown sugar, chili sauce and undrained peaches. Blend until smooth.
- Place pork loin in a heavy plastic bag; pour on half of peach sauce. Refrigerate, covered, overnight. Refrigerate remaining peach sauce.
- Prepare grill by arranging a drip pan surrounded by medium hot coals (if using gas grill, heat to medium temperature).
- Add hickory chips, dampened with water, to heat source.
- Place pork, meat thermometer inserted, on grill over drip pan. Baste often with marinade until internal temperature reaches 155 degrees, about 45-60 minutes.
- Let stand 10 minutes, allowing internal temperature to rise to 160 degrees.
- Slice thinly and serve with reserved peach sauce, heated.
- Serves 6-8.

AN EARLY CATTLE BARON

One of the most successful ranchers in early day Colorado was John W. Iliff. He had contracts with the army and the railroad construction camps to supply them with cattle to feed the soldiers and workers. At the height of his empire he controlled 650,000 acres. He could feed more than 30,000 head, and sell them at a profit. He handled his vast acreage through the use of cow camps. These consisted of men, horses, a sod hut, water and other supplies spread strategically across Iliff's domain. Camps of this type spread the tools of the cowboys trade into Colorado forevermore. Unfortunately, Iliff did not live long enough to enjoy his success as he died suddenly in 1878.

Stuffed Beef Bundles

1 (7.5 oz) pkg stuffing mix

1 env onion soup mix

¼ tsp pepper

⅔ (12 oz) can evaporated milk

2 lbs Maverick Ranch NaturaLite Beef Ground Round

2 (10.75 oz) cans cream of mushroom soup

⅓ cup ketchup

4 tbsp F & J Worcestershire Sauce

- Prepare stuffing according to pkg directions.
- Mix soup mix, pepper, milk and beef until combined.
- Divide meat into 8 equal portions, place on waxed paper and pat into 6″ circles.
- Place ¼ cup of stuffing in center of each patty, pull meat over stuffing on all sides and seal edges.
- Place patties seam side down in 13″ x 9″ baking dish.
- Mix mushroom soup, ketchup and Worcestershire sauce until blended. Pour evenly over bundles.
- Bake at 350 degrees for 20 minutes.
- Serves 4-6.

Italian Sausage Stuffed Bell Peppers

4-6 green, yellow or red bell peppers
1 medium onion, chopped
1 tbsp vegetable oil
1 lb Old West Italian Sausage
1 cup cooked rice or diced cooked potatoes
1 cup shredded mozzarella cheese
1 jar Aiello's Spaghetti Sauce
water

- Stem and core bell peppers; remove white membranes and wash thoroughly.
- Sauté onion in oil in heavy skillet until translucent.
- Add sausage and cook completely.
- Add the rice or potatoes and ¾ cup mozzarella; mix well.
- Stuff the peppers with the meat mixture; place in 2 qt casserole dish.
- Pour ⅓ of spaghetti sauce over the peppers. Add 1″ water to pan, cover and place in 350 degree oven for 30-45 minutes.
- Heat the remaining spaghetti sauce; pour over cooked peppers.
- Garnish with remaining cheese.
- Serves 4-6.

Corned Beef With Honey Mustard Sauce

2-4 lbs seasoned Temptee Brand Corned Beef
water
½ cup butter or margarine
½ cup Ambrosia Honey
½ cup Colorado Gold Mustard
1 tbsp curry

- Place corned beef in Dutch oven and cover with water.
- Bake at 300 degrees 2-3 hours or until tender. Pour off excess water.
- Heat remaining ingredients; pour over corned beef. Return to oven and bake 30 minutes more.
- Serves 3-5.

VICTORIAN LEGACY

As one travels throughout the state, a type of attraction that is truly a treasure may not be noted in travel brochures, but it is waiting to be enjoyed in almost every town in the state. This treasure is Victorian architecture. The riches generated by the mining activity during the 1800s in Colorado provided the state with the largest collection of Victorian mansions of any state in the Rockies. Scott Warren and Beth Lambertson Warren researched and documented this unsung treasure in their book, Victorian Bonanza: Victorian Architecture of the Rocky Mountain West. Most of the architecture was designed by enterprising Easterners who traveled west to settle a wild frontier.

Marinated Flank Steak

¼ cup Honeyville Honey
¼ cup low sodium soy sauce
1½ tsp ginger
1 clove garlic, crushed or minced
2 green onions, minced
2 tbsp wine vinegar
⅔ cup vegetable oil
1 (1½ lb) Maverick Ranch NaturaLite Beef Flank Steak

- Mix all ingredients of marinade together.
- Marinate steak for 6 hours or overnight. Turn meat occasionally.
- Cook on grill or barbecue, basting with marinade.
- After steak is cooked to desired doneness, slice on a diagonal.
- Serves 4.

Best Brisket

½ cup Graham's Golden Honey
½ cup low sodium soy sauce
⅔ cup Naturally Nuts Peanut Butter
5 tbsp Dijon mustard
1 clove garlic, minced
2 green onions with tops, chopped
1 (3-4 lb) Maverick Ranch NaturaLite Beef Brisket

- Mix first 6 ingredients.
- Place brisket on a large piece of heavy duty aluminum foil in baking pan. Cover with sauce. Fold foil over brisket and tightly seal.
- Cook in slow oven 275 degrees for 5 hours.
- Thinly slice and serve with sauce.
- Serves 6-8.

Barbecued Brisket

1 (2½-3 lb) Colorado Beef Brisket

1 tsp onion salt

1 tsp garlic salt

1 tsp celery salt

¾ cup F & J Mesquite Worcestershire Sauce

F & J Bar B Q Sauce, to taste

- Rub sides of brisket with seasonings.
- Marinate in Worcestershire sauce overnight in shallow baking pan covered and sealed with aluminum foil. Do not open.
- Place in 200 degree oven for 6-8 hours.
- Drain marinade off completely. Pour barbecue sauce over brisket and return to 350 degree oven, uncovered. Cook 15 minutes on each side; add barbecue sauce after turning brisket.
- Cool completely before slicing, then reheat if desired.
- Serves 6-8.

Pork Tenderloin Diane

1 lb Colorado Pork Tenderloin, cut into 8 crosswise pieces

2 tsp lemon pepper

2 tbsp butter

2 tbsp lemon juice

1 tbsp F & J Worcestershire Sauce

1 tsp Dijon mustard

1 tbsp minced Bellwether Farms Parsley or Chives

- Press each tenderloin slice to a 1" thickness. Sprinkle surfaces of medallions with lemon pepper.
- Heat butter in heavy skillet; cook tenderloin medallions 3-4 minutes on each side.
- Remove medallions to serving platter; keep warm.
- Add lemon juice, Worcestershire sauce and mustard to skillet. Cook, stirring with pan juices, until heated thoroughly.
- Pour sauce over medallions, sprinkle with parsley or chives and serve.
- Serves 4.

FIRST IN COLORADO

Here are a few firsts in Colorado history: 1540, Coronado moves into the area on a grand expedition, and Plains Indians see horses for the first time; 1861, William Gilpin appoints the first Territorial Governor; 1874, the Colorado School of Mines opens; 1877, the University of Colorado opens; 1883, first electric lights installed in Denver; 1886, the Denver Union Stockyards are established; 1894, the Colorado State Capitol is completed; 1899, the first sugar beet refinery is built; 1904, the U.S. Mint issues its first coins; 1910, the first airplane flies into Denver; 1922, the first commercial radio license is issued to a Colorado outlet.

Lemon and Mustard Baked Chicken

¼ cup Rocky Mountain Butter
1 large clove garlic, minced
2 tbsp Colorado Gold Mustard
1 cup dry bread crumbs
2 tsp grated lemon peel
½ tsp crumbled, dried tarragon
4 chicken breast halves
salt and pepper

- Preheat oven to 350 degrees.
- Line baking pan with foil.
- Melt butter in heavy medium skillet over low heat.
- Add garlic; sauté 1 minute.
- Remove from heat; stir in mustard.
- Mix bread crumbs, lemon peel and tarragon on waxed paper.
- Turn chicken in butter mixture to coat, then turn in crumbs, coating completely.
- Arrange in prepared pan, sprinkle with salt and pepper.
- Bake until chicken is cooked thoroughly, basting with pan drippings, about 1 hour.
- Place a piece of foil loosely on top for first half hour, to prevent browning too quickly.
- Serves 4.

GETTING TO KNOW COLORADO

Colorado, the Centennial State, joined the Union in 1876, just as the nation was celebrating its Centennial. The state's name came from the Spanish word for "red" or "muddy", a reference to the Colorado River. The state flower is the Rocky Mountain columbine; state tree the Colorado Blue Spruce; state bird the lark bunting; and the state animal is the Rocky Mountain bighorn sheep. Its land mass is an area of 104,247 square miles with altitudes ranging from 3,350 to 14,431 feet above sea level. Population: over 3 million. Seasons of the year are subtle. Summers don't bring endless days of excessive heat nor extensive cloudy or dreary spells. Rather, most days are pleasantly cool, while winters are mild with more sunshine than the summer months. Small wonder that most people who visit call Colorado America's favorite vacationland.

Golden Barbecued Spare Ribs

2½ lbs Cedaredge Pork Spare Ribs
1 medium OGI Onion, sliced
1 tbsp vegetable oil
4 Colorado Golden Delicious Apples
1 cup ketchup
1¼ cups water
1 tbsp brown sugar
1 tbsp lemon juice
½ tsp salt

- Cut spare ribs into serving pieces; place in single layer in baking pan.
- Bake at 500 degrees 30 minutes, until browned. Remove from oven; drain off drippings.
- While ribs brown, sauté onion in oil until tender.
- Peel, core and grate 2 apples.
- Add to onion along with ketchup, water, sugar, lemon juice and salt. Simmer 15 minutes.
- Spoon over browned ribs. Cover; bake at 325 degrees 1½ hours.
- Core and quarter remaining 2 apples. Arrange in pan with meat.
- Cover; bake 30 minutes longer or until apples are tender.
- Serves 4-6.

FAST TRACKS

Harbingers of civilization—the railroads—were wild and woolly Colorado's link to Eastern cities, workers and money. They played a vital role in the settlement of the West, and no less in Colorado.

The name which stands out is General William Jackson Palmer. In 1869 he was hired by the Kansas Pacific to survey rail routes to Denver. He did this and later handled the construction of the new route. Palmer decided he wanted to build his own railroad, to border the Front Range south from Denver.

Thus, in 1870, the Denver and Rio Grande Railroad was begun. Construction of the rails began in 1871, moving quickly to Colorado City and Pueblo and continuing to El Moro just outside Trinidad. However, the Santa Fe Railroad, moving west, met the Denver and Rio Grande at El Moro, and, in a crafty move, was able to begin laying track south of El Moro before the D&RG, which then abandoned its efforts to move south.

Glazed-Corned Beef

2-4 lbs seasoned Temptee Brand Corned Beef

water

½ cup GW Dark Brown Sugar

½ tsp cloves

½ tsp ginger

½ tsp dry mustard

1 tbsp sesame seeds

- Place corned beef in a pot and cover with water.
- Bring to boil; cover, lower heat and simmer slowly for 2-3 hours, or until tender. Drain.
- Blend together remaining ingredients and rub into meat while still warm.
- Roast corned beef over a slow charcoal fire 15 minutes. Continue to brush corned beef with glaze until done.
- Serves 3-5.

Boeuf Bourguignonne

3 tbsp olive oil

3 lbs Colorado Beef Round Steak, cut in 1½" cubes

1 large carrot, peeled and sliced

1 medium onion, sliced

½ tsp salt

⅛ tsp pepper

3 tbsp all-purpose flour

1 (10.5 oz) can condensed beef broth

1 tbsp Cream of the Valley Tomato Paste

2 cloves garlic, minced

1 tsp whole thyme

1 small whole bay leaf

6 boiling onions, peeled

½ lb Rakhra Mushrooms, sliced

½ cup Pikes Peak Vineyards Colorado Red Wine

- Heat 1 tbsp olive oil in skillet; add beef cubes and brown well.
- Place browned beef cubes in slow cooker.
- Brown carrot and onion in skillet. Season with salt and pepper; stir in flour.
- Add broth, mix well and add to slow cooker.
- Add tomato paste, garlic, thyme, bay leaf and onions. Cover and cook on low 8-10 hours.
- Sauté mushrooms in remaining 2 tbsp olive oil and add with wine to slow cooker about 1 hour before serving.
- Serves 4-6.

Pepper Steak

1 (2-3 lb) beef round steak

2 tbsp Dixon & Sons Q-Mix

¾ cup Hungarian® Flour

1 (8 oz) can tomato sauce

1 large Tatey's Best Onion, sliced

1 bell pepper, sliced

½ cup Dixon & Sons Steak Sauce

- Cut steak into bite-size pieces. Sprinkle with mix.
- Shake steak in bag with flour. Pan fry in Dutch oven.
- Stir in tomato sauce, onion, pepper and steak sauce.
- Place covered in 350 degree oven for 1 hour.
- Serves 4-6.

DESSERTS

Skiing Breckenridge

Photo courtesy of the Breckenridge Ski Corporation

BAKING UP HIGH

Avoiding falling cakes in the mountains can be easy as avoiding falling rocks. Here are some standard adjustments: Bake shortened cakes at 400 degrees to help set the structure rapidly. Decrease baking powder by between one-eighth and one-fourth above 5,000 feet. Decrease sugar by one tablespoon per cup in the recipe from 3,000 to 5,000 feet, and as much as three tablespoons per cup from 5,000 to 7,000 feet or higher. This helps to strengthen structure and prevent cakes from falling.

To compensate for moisture loss, liquid can be increased by one tablespoon per cup of liquid at 3,000 feet and up to four tablespoons per cup at 7,000 feet. It may also be necessary to reduce fat by one to two tablespoons per cup to strengthen structure. Beat egg whites slightly less at high altitudes to avoid trapping too much air, (only until peaks fall over instead of stiff and dry).

Chocolate Marshmallow Torte

½ lb chocolate almond bars
1 cup Meadow Gold Milk
22 marshmallows
1 pt Meadow Gold Old Style Heavy Whip Cream
32 graham crackers, rolled fine
½ cup sugar
½ cup melted Meadow Gold Butter

- Break chocolate bars into small pieces; melt in top of double boiler with milk and marshmallows.
- Whip cream and fold into first mixture when it has cooled.
- Mix together graham cracker crumbs, sugar and melted butter.
- Line greased 8" x 12" pan with graham cracker crust mixture, reserving excess.
- Pour chocolate mixture into crust.
- Put remaining crumb mixture over the top.
- Chill. Cut into bars.
- Makes 40-45 bars.

ON VAIL MOUNTAIN

The Colorado Ski Museum holds a prime spot between Vail Village and Lionshead, two of the areas which serve the visitor in this mountain community. Winter and summer a gondola will take you to the upper regions of Vail Mountain where you can enjoy a good meal, then ski or hike down depending upon the season.

Of course, hiking and biking are exceptionally popular with well-marked trails for both, winding around the mountain or along the valley floor. Golf, tennis, lacrosse, rugby, rafting, ice skating—the list of sporting possibilities seems endless. And when the day is over just watching the sun set over the Rockies or the moonlight off the face of the mountain is enough to bring you back for more.

Luscious Gain-A-Pound Cake

2½ cups sifted Hungarian®
All-Purpose Flour
1 tsp baking powder
½ tsp salt
1 cup Robinson Butter
1¼ cups Holly Granulated Sugar
1¼ tsp Rodelle Vanilla
4 eggs
½ cup brewed, dark roasted Boyer's
Gourmet Coffee

- Preheat oven to 325 degrees.
- Combine dry ingredients and sift into a large bowl.
- In a separate bowl, cream butter until soft and fluffy.
- Add sugar, 2 tbsp at a time, creaming thoroughly after each addition.
- Add vanilla and blend well.
- Beat in eggs, 1 at a time.
- Add coffee and flour mixture, blending well.
- Line a 9" x 5" loaf pan with waxed paper.
- Pour mixture into loaf pan; bake 1 hour, 25 minutes.
- Remove from oven; let stand 15 minutes.
- Turn out on a rack to cool.
- Serves 16.

"Taste of Colorado," State Capitol, Denver

Photo by Jeff Andrew

CITY OF METALS

"When I walk down a Denver street, I always feel as if I were listening to a brass band," one distinguished visitor to the city is quoted as saying. Whether or not you hear the band, you will surely hear the tinkle of coins by visiting the United States Mint in Denver and watching money being made anytime throughout the year.

Or look up to see metal in another form. It's only appropriate that the state capitol in Denver would be capped by a golden dome. What else in a state where gold was so vital to development? It also seems appropriate that in this land of altitude the capital city is exactly one mile above sea level.

Mile High Fudge

2 cups Holly Brown Sugar
1 cup Holly Granulated Sugar
1 cup evaporated milk
½ cup Meadow Gold Butter
1 (7 oz) jar marshmallow cream
1 (6 oz) pkg milk chocolate chips
1 (6 oz) pkg semi-sweet chocolate chips
½ cup chopped walnuts
1 tsp vanilla

- Combine sugars, milk and butter in saucepan. Bring to full boil over moderate heat, stirring constantly.
- Boil 15 minutes, stirring occasionally, being careful not to scrape sugar crystals down from sides of saucepan. (This may cause the fudge to become grainy).
- Remove from heat. Add marshmallow cream and chocolate chips, stirring until mixture is smooth.
- Blend in chopped walnuts and vanilla.
- Pour into greased 9" square pan. Chill until firm.
- Makes 2½ lbs.

High Altitude Adjustments:
- 5,000 ft: Add 1 tbsp evaporated milk. Boil 16 minutes.
- 8,000 ft and over: Add 2 tbsp evaporated milk. Boil 16½-17 minutes.

THE CHILDREN'S MUSEUM OF DENVER

One could not discuss a trip to Denver without mentioning The Children's Museum. Built from the foundation up with children in mind it provides a constantly changing environment meant to stimulate and challenge the young. Some of the best exhibits never change, such as the thousands of plastic balls children dive and sink into for hours. Other exhibits change regularly. Next time you are there you may find that you can shoot baskets, or measure yourself against photographs of professional basketball players, or try your hand at making up your face like a lion or clown, or finding out about caring for your teeth, or even constructing a house. And then again, maybe none of these will be there and an array of new exhibits will be in place for your visit.

Apricot Bread Pudding

8 Leroux Creek Dried Apricot Halves

4 slices Earth Grains Very Thin Sandwich White Bread

1¼ cups Royal Crest Lowfat Milk

3 eggs

1 tsp vanilla

½ tsp almond extract

¼ tsp salt

2½ tbsp Lucky Clover Honey

1 tsp grated orange rind

boiling water

- Put 1 apricot half into each of 4 oven-proof cups.
- Crumple 1 slice of bread into each cup.
- Put 1 more apricot half into each cup.
- In blender, combine milk, eggs, flavorings, salt, honey and orange rind. Divide mixture evenly among cups.
- Place cups in 8" x 8" pan; pour in boiling water to depth of 1½".
- Bake at 350 degrees 35-40 minutes.
- Serves 4.

ONE WAY TO KNOW BOULDER

Among other sites in Boulder is a Victorian house set not far off one of the main streets in the city. The notoriety of the house can best be summed up in the story of a traveler to the Soviet Union who stopped to visit with a young boy there.

In their halting conversation the traveler indicated he was from Boulder, Colorado. He asked the boy if he knew anything about this distant city. The boy immediately responded, "Nanu, Nanu." Those words were used constantly in a once-popular American television program, "Mork and Mindy," which was, in fact, set in Boulder, Colorado in that very Victorian house.

Classic Butter Cookies

1½ cups Meadow Gold Butter
1 cup GW Granulated Sugar
1 egg
2 tsp Rodelle Vanilla
¼ tsp salt
4½ cups Wheat Land Farms All-Purpose Flour

- Preheat oven to 375 degrees.
- Beat butter, sugar, egg, vanilla and salt in large mixer bowl until light and fluffy.
- Gradually add flour; beat until well mixed.
- Cover dough; refrigerate 1 hour.
- Work with ¼ dough at a time; keep remaining dough chilled.
- Roll out on lightly floured surface to ¼" thickness.
- Cut or mold dough into desired shapes.
- Repeat with remaining dough.
- Place cookies on unbuttered baking sheets.
- Bake 8-10 minutes, or until cookies are lightly browned.
- Remove cookies to rack; cool completely.
- Store in airtight containers at room temperature.
- Makes 4-6 doz cookies.

THE STATE'S FIRST BUSINESS

Bent's Fort on the Arkansas River. It was the Macy's of Indians come to trade buffalo robes for beads, bells and calico. It was the Grand Central Station for travelers from both ends of the one thousand-mile Santa Fe Trail. And Bent's Fort Lightning refreshed the thirst of many a prospector and trapper. It was the first large business enterprise in Colorado, built between LaJunta and Las Animas by William and Charles Bent and Ceran St. Vrain.

Chocolate Raspberry Bars

½ cup unsalted butter, softened
¾ cup GW Granulated Sugar
1 egg, separated
½ tsp vanilla
¾ cup plus 1 tbsp Wheat Land Farms All-Purpose Flour
¼ cup cocoa
⅛ tsp salt
¼ cup Gingerbear House Raspberry Jam
¼ cup chopped walnuts
2 tbsp GW Granulated Sugar, to decorate

- Cream butter and sugar until light and fluffy.
- Add egg yolk and vanilla, beating until thick and silky.
- Sift together flour, cocoa and salt; add to creamed mixture, stirring just until moistened.
- Spread in ungreased 8" x 8" baking pan. Chill in freezer 10 minutes.
- Heat oven to 350 degrees.
- Stir jam and spread over chilled dough; return to freezer to chill an additional 5 minutes.
- Beat egg white until frothy.
- Brush half over chilled raspberry jam; discarding the rest.
- Scatter nuts on top and lightly press in place.
- Bake in oven 20-25 minutes.
- Mixture is done when edges begin to pull away from sides of pan.
- Remove from oven; sprinkle immediately with 2 tbsp sugar for topping.
- Cool in pan before cutting.
- Makes 30-35 bars.

PUEBLO AND TRINIDAD

Pueblo and Trinidad, two southern Colorado towns with rich histories dating back to the mid-1800s, are stops for the curious. Both have museums and monuments dedicated to their pasts. The Pueblo Depot, a vital installation in our country's defense, is available for touring on special request. Also the Ludlow Massacre monument in nearby Trinidad commemorating a dark period in union/management relations is available for touring.

Neapolitan Ice Cream Pie

Brownie Crust:

½ cup Rocky Mountain Butter

1 cup Holly Granulated Sugar

2 eggs, separated

2 (1 oz) squares unsweetened baking chocolate, melted and cooled

1 tsp vanilla

½ cup all-purpose flour

⅛ tsp salt

Filling:

2 pts Likity Split Strawberry Ice Cream, softened

1 cup Royal Crest Whipping Cream

2 tbsp Holly Powdered Sugar

½ tsp vanilla

¼ tsp almond extract

½ cup sliced almonds, toasted

- Preheat oven to 325 degrees.
- For brownie crust, cream butter and sugar until light and fluffy.
- Add egg yolks; mix well.
- Stir in chocolate and vanilla.
- Blend in flour and salt.
- Beat egg whites until soft peaks form; fold into chocolate mixture. Spread batter in a buttered 9″ pie plate.
- Bake 30-35 minutes, or until a wooden pick inserted in center comes out clean.
- Remove from heat. Cool completely.
- Spread ice cream in "well" of crust. Return to freezer 2-3 hours, or until firm.
- Combine whipping cream, sugar and extracts; whip until stiff.
- Fold in almonds. Spread over ice cream.
- Serve immediately, or return to freezer. If freezing, let pie stand at room temperature 15-20 minutes before serving.
- Serves 6-8.

CRESTED BUTTE: HIDDEN TREASURES

Crested Butte is unique in Colorado, and unlike many areas, the mining industry never really did die here; molybdenum is still mined. Tucked away high in the Elk Mountains, Crested Butte not only attracts skiers but hikers and fishermen as well. There's also an excellent golf course. The town of Crested Butte has been designated as a National Historic District and it is well maintained. The village serving the ski area is a couple of miles outside Crested Butte but is connected by a shuttle service. Shoppers report that you can get some real bargins in Crested Butte.

Cajeta de Cafe

¾ cup GW Granulated Sugar

4 eggs

2 egg yolks

½ cup firmly packed GW Dark Brown Sugar

1 (15 oz) can condensed milk

1 cup brewed cold, strong Boyer's Coffee

- Preheat oven to 375 degrees.
- Place granulated sugar in a square or round flat-bottomed casserole that can be used over direct heat and in the oven.
- Over low heat, stir until sugar dissolves to a golden syrup. Remove from heat.
- With pot holders, rotate casserole to coat bottom with caramelized sugar. Set aside until completely cool.
- Combine remaining ingredients in blender; blend until smooth. Pour into caramel-lined casserole.
- Place casserole in a large baking pan and pour in hot water about halfway up outside of casserole. Bake in preheated oven 1 hour or until a knife inserted near center comes out clean.
- Cool to room temperature. Refrigerate until chilled.
- Serve in dessert glasses; spoon some of the sauce from the bottom of the casserole over each serving.
- Serves 6-8.

Denver City Pudding Cake

¾ cup Hungarian® All-Purpose Flour

3 tsp baking powder

⅛ tsp salt

¾ cup sugar

½ cup fine dry bread crumbs, divided

3 tbsp butter

3 tbsp cocoa

1 egg, slightly beaten

⅓ cup Graves Dairy Milk, at room temperature

½ tsp vanilla

¾ cup firmly packed GW Brown Sugar

¼ cup more cocoa

1½ cups brewed strong Boyer's Coffee, at room temperature

vanilla ice cream or whipped cream

- Preheat oven to 350 degrees. Generously butter a 9″ square baking pan; set aside.
- Sift together flour, baking powder and salt into a medium bowl.
- Stir in sugar and ¼ cup bread crumbs.
- In a small saucepan, melt butter.
- Stir in cocoa; continue stirring until smooth.
- Remove from heat. Cool slightly.
- Stir in egg; add milk. Stir until smooth.
- Stir in vanilla.
- Stir cocoa-milk mixture into flour mixture; blend well. Pour into prepared pan.
- Sift brown sugar over surface; sprinkle with remaining bread crumbs and cocoa. Do not stir or mix.
- Carefully pour coffee over all. Again, do not stir or mix.
- Bake 40-45 minutes, or until top is crusty. Do not chill.
- Serve warm or at room temperature with vanilla ice cream or chilled whipped cream.
- Serves 6-8.

HIGH COUNTRY HIGHWAYS

Mount Evans Highway winds upward from Idaho Springs, moving past high country slopes that are a refuge for big horn sheep, elk, deer, and mountain lion. The road slips through great stands of aspen, evergreen and bristle cone pines. At 14,260 feet, it is the highest paved highway in North America. However, the Virginia Canyon Highway that cuts between Idaho Springs and Central City just may be the most memorable route in the state. It is only nine miles long. But those are nine spectacular, white-knuckled miles, jutting past old mines, the famous Glory Hole, and what's left of the town of Russell Gulch. And when you look down at the hairpen curves, you will immediately know why it has always been called the "Oh My Gawd Road."

Old Style Buttermilk Brownies

2 cups sugar

2 cups Horizon All-Purpose Flour

4 tbsp cocoa

1 cup cold water

½ cup Meadow Gold Butter

½ cup vegetable oil

½ cup Meadow Gold Old Style Buttermilk

1 tsp baking soda

2 eggs

walnuts (optional)

- Sift sugar, flour and cocoa together in large bowl.
- In saucepan, bring water, butter and oil to boil. Pour over dry ingredients.
- Add buttermilk, baking soda and eggs.
- Top batter with walnuts, if desired.
- Bake in 15½" x 10½" x 1" jelly roll pan in 400 degree oven 18-20 minutes.
- Makes 45-50 brownies.

BROADMOOR OPENING

"Requesting your presence at the formal opening of The Broadmoor, Colorado Springs June 29, 1918 Dinner at eight o'clock Dancing".

Such was the invitation to what Colorado Springs' leading newspaper called "the largest, most glittering gala social event of the town's whole 47 year history."

Spencer Penrose had seen his vision become reality. Penrose, made fabulously wealthy by the Cripple Creek gold strike, was a frequent traveler and frequenter of some of the world's most famous hotels and spas. He obviously thought of owning one of his own in which everything would be built and maintained to his liking.

The machinations to acquire the site for the hotel, its construction and promotion and the involvement of Penrose and his close associates in nearly every detail could fill a book by itself.

Never Fail Chocolate Cake

2 cups Wheat Land Farms All-Purpose Flour

2 cups GW Granulated Sugar

2 tsp baking soda

½ cup cocoa

¼ tsp salt

1 cup vegetable oil

1 cup Meadow Gold Old Style Buttermilk

2 eggs

1 cup hot water

- Preheat oven to 350 degrees.
- Sift dry ingredients into bowl.
- Add oil and buttermilk.
- Beat with mixer; add eggs and beat again.
- Add hot water, beating slowly.
- Bake in 13" x 9" pan 35-40 minutes.
- Makes 24-30 servings.

THE HOUSE THAT MOLLY BUILT

In poking around Denver, drive over to 1340 Pennsylvania Street for a tour of the Molly Brown House. Built around 1890 it's situated in Denver's Capitol Hill area. Turn-of-the-century and Victorian influences set the decor, and Margaret Tobin Brown added other ideas from her frequent trips to Europe. But, the real story of the house was its occupant—"The Unsinkable Molly Brown."

Although Molly is now pointed to as one of Denver's most famous residents, she wasn't always so well regarded. After marrying J.J. Brown in Leadville, and reaping with him the benefits from his mining interests, Molly moved to Denver and tried to enter Denver society. No deal. However, when Molly showed great heroism as she left the sinking Titanic in 1912, Denver's society matrons relented and she became a fixture.

It wasn't until many years after her death that she really became a Colorado folk hero. That was when the Broadway musical "The Unsinkable Molly Brown" opened to rave reviews and became an international success, later being translated into a motion picture of the same name.

Maple Pecan Frozen Yoghurt

4 cups Mountain High® Plain Yoghurt

1 cup chopped Naturally Nuts Pecans, toasted

1 cup pure maple syrup

- In large bowl, combine ingredients; mix well.
- Pour into 1½ qt or larger ice cream freezer container.
- Freeze according to manufacturer's instructions.
- Makes 6 cups.

Colorado Pear Sorbet

¾ cup Pikes Peak Vineyards Colorado White Wine

1½ tbsp lemon juice

⅓ cup sugar

5 small Colorado Pears, peeled, cored and sliced

- In a small saucepan, combine all ingredients.
- Bring to a boil over high heat; cover, reduce heat and simmer 8-10 minutes, or until pears are tender.
- Pour mixture into a food processor; blend until pureed.
- Pour mixture into a shallow pan; freeze until solid.
- When frozen, remove from freezer; let stand at room temperature until the mixture can be broken into chunks with a spoon.
- Put chunks in the food processor; mix until the consistency of slush.
- Pour mixture into a freezer container or individual serving dishes; return to freezer until firm. The sorbet can be kept in an airtight container for up to 2 months.
- Serves 6.

Healthy Cookies

1 cup Rocky Mountain Butter, softened

½ cup Ambrosia Honey

2 eggs, slightly beaten

2½ cups Wheat Land Farms Whole Wheat Flour

¼ tsp salt (optional)

5 tbsp Geronimo Tea

1 cup chopped Mrs. Sutler's Walnuts

½ cup Leroux Creek Raisins

- Cream butter and honey; add eggs.
- Sift together flour, salt and tea. Add slowly to butter mixture, mixing well.
- Add walnuts and raisins.
- Drop by teaspoonfuls on cookie sheet.
- Bake in 375 degree oven for 10-15 minutes.
- Makes 2 doz cookies.

"LITTLE WHITE MAN"

William Bent had come into the territory as an employee of the American Fur Company at the age of 15, thus acquiring the name Little White Man from the Indians. Though his brother Charles left the trading post and went on to become the first territorial governor of New Mexico, William continued the Fort's commerce. But with business becoming less profitable each year, he tried to sell the fort to the U.S. government. Unfortunately, negotiations dragged on for some time, so, an independent character to the end, Bent packed his goods and blew up the fort. Today's traveler has the opportunity to view the fort in its reconstructed glory; it's a National Historic Site.

Microwaved Sour Cream Apple Pie

4 Colorado Apples, cored, peeled and sliced

⅔ cup GW Granulated Sugar

1 tbsp Wheat Land Farms All-Purpose Flour

½ tsp cinnamon

dash nutmeg

½ cup Meadow Gold Sour Cream

1, 9" baked pastry shell

Crumb Mixture:

¾ cup Wheat Land Farms All-Purpose Flour

⅓ cup packed GW Brown Sugar

½ tsp cinnamon

dash nutmeg

¼ cup Meadow Gold Butter

- Combine first 6 ingredients.
- Spoon evenly into pastry shell.
- Make crumb mixture by combining flour, brown sugar, cinnamon and nutmeg; cut in butter until crumbly. Top apples completely.
- Microwave pie, elevated on a rack, on HIGH power, uncovered 7½-8½ minutes, or until apples are tender.
- Serve hot or cold.
- Serves 6-8.

DENVER'S BOULDER CONNECTION

There's good argument for saying that Denver is now becoming Denver-Boulder, for the corridor between the state capitol and the home of the University of Colorado is sprouting small businesses, hotels, shopping centers and restaurants nearly connecting the two cities.

Boulder is unique in Colorado. Besides housing the University of Colorado, it also boasts several major hi-tech companies and a thriving retail community. Its open space concept has left ample room for hikers, joggers and bikers to roam the areas around and in the towering Flatirons, which is what the "leftover" rocks from the Ancestral Rockies are called in Boulder.

Chautauqua Park is a flourishing remnant of the time in America when Chautauqua meetings were held throughout the land, with the Chautauqua Hall still remaining and in use as a restaurant. The area is also the site for summer concerts, films and lectures.

Butter Almond Toffee Pie

1 (8 oz) bar chocolate almond candy
16 marshmallows
½ cup Royal Crest Milk
1 (8 oz) ctn whipped topping
1, 8" graham cracker pie shell
1 cup Vern's Butter Almond Toffee, crushed

- Melt chocolate and marshmallows with milk in a double boiler; cool.
- Fold in whipped topping.
- Pile into pie crust.
- Cover with crushed toffee.
- Chill in refrigerator at least 4 hours before serving.
- Serves 6-8.

GENTEEL GEORGETOWN

Today's Georgetown is an interesting stop for sightseeing, eating, shopping and a step into a Colorado gold rush area which has always had a somewhat genteel air about it. That was primarily due to the efforts of one man, the mysterious Frenchman, Louis Dupuy. He began his life in Georgetown as a miner, later saving a fellow miner's life, but being injured in the effort. He was rewarded with a purse of money by the Georgetown citizens, which led to his development of the famous Hotel de Paris. For many years it served as the center of social activities in Georgetown.

Frozen Hawaiian Pie

1⅓ cups flaked coconut, toasted
1½ cups vanilla wafer crumbs
½ cup melted Meadow Gold Butter
1 (8 oz) pkg Neufchatel cheese, softened
1 cup Mountain High® Honey
Vanilla Yoghurt
1 (8 oz) can juice-packed crushed
pineapple, well drained
¼ cup frozen pineapple-orange juice
concentrate, thawed
2 tbsp Lucky Clover Honey
1 tsp grated orange rind
⅓ cup chopped macadamia nuts
1 cup Meadow Gold Whipping Cream,
whipped

- To toast coconut, spread on cookie sheet and bake in 350 degree oven until browned.
- Reserve ½ cup coconut; combine remaining coconut, crumbs and butter.
- Press into buttered 9″ pie plate; bake at 350 degrees 8 minutes.
- Beat cheese until fluffy; beat in remaining ingredients except whipped cream.
- Chill ½ hour; fold in whipped cream.
- Turn into crust. Freeze 6 hours or until firm.
- Remove from freezer ½ hour before serving.
- Serves 6-8.

ATOP PIKES PEAK

On top of Pikes Peak, near Colorado Springs, the plains spread 125 miles eastward to the Kansas border. To the west, the snow-crowned Continental Divide rides skyward. North and South, big mountains shoulder the distant horizon. Gazing upon this colossal expanse, you will understand how Katherine Lee Bates, on the summit of Pikes Peak in 1893, was inspired to compose "America the Beautiful."

Pike's Peak Peach Cobbler

3 cups sliced Colorado Peaches

¼ cup plus 3 tbsp Holly Granulated Sugar

1 tbsp lemon juice

1 tsp grated lemon peel

1 tsp almond extract

Dough:

1½ cups Wheat Land Farms All-Purpose Flour

½ tsp salt

1 tbsp baking powder

3 tbsp Holly Granulated Sugar

⅓ cup shortening

½ cup Graves Dairy Milk

1 egg

- Arrange peaches in well buttered 8" square pan or deep casserole; sprinkle with mixture of ¼ cup sugar, lemon juice, lemon peel and almond extract.
- Heat peaches in 375 degree oven while preparing dough.
- Combine flour, salt, baking powder and 1 tbsp sugar; cut in shortening until crumbly.
- Add milk and egg; stir just until well moistened.
- Spoon small dollops of dough over hot peaches and spread dough; sprinkle with 2 tbsp sugar.
- Continue baking in 375 degree oven 40 minutes.
- Serves 6.

High Altitude Adjustments:

- 5,000 ft: Decrease granulated sugar to ¼ cup plus 1tbsp. Increase flour by 2 tbsp. Decrease baking powder to 2¼ tsp.
- 8,000 ft and over: Decrease granulated sugar to ¼ cup plus 1 tbsp. Increase flour by 2 tbsp. Decrease baking powder to 2 tsp.

CONQUERING A MOUNTAIN

Ski slopes exist throughout Colorado, and you will get an argument from inveterate skiers as to which is the best or the toughest. Whether you frequent one of the Front Range ski areas, or visit the destination point areas, you will discover a broad range of conditions and terrain. Wherever you go, though, you will find great effort put into the care of the slopes and the safety of the skier. Most people think of Colorado only as a downhill skier's paradise. But many "skinny" skiers (or cross-country skiers) abound, and this version of the sport is one of the best ways to see the back country.

Baur's Famous Mija Pie

1 cup sugar

4 tbsp cornstarch

¼ tsp salt

2 cups Graves Dairy Milk, divided

2 egg yolks

4½ tbsp cocoa

2 (1 oz) squares sweet baking chocolate, grated

1 tbsp butter

½ tsp vanilla

1, 9" baked pie shell

½ cup ground Andre's Old Fashioned Colorado Almond Toffee Candy

- Combine sugar, cornstarch and salt.
- Add ¼ cup milk, mixing well.
- Blend in egg yolks.
- Scald 1½ cups milk in saucepan over moderate heat.
- Whisk in cornstarch mixture until smooth.
- Continue to cook, whisking, until clear and thickened.
- Dissolve cocoa in remaining ¼ cup milk.
- Whisk cocoa mixture and grated chocolate into cornstarch mixture.
- Cook, whisking, until chocolate melts and mixture is thickened.
- Remove from heat, add butter and vanilla. Stir until butter melts.
- Refrigerate until thoroughly chilled.
- Turn into baked pie shell.
- Sprinkle ground candy over top.
- Refrigerate until chilled.
- Serves 6-8.

Pinto Fiesta Cake

1 cup GW Granulated Sugar
¼ cup butter
1 egg, beaten
2 cups cooked Pantry Pinto Beans, mashed
1 cup Hungarian® All-Purpose Flour
1 tsp baking soda
½ tsp salt
1 tsp cinnamon
½ tsp cloves
½ tsp allspice
2 cups diced raw Colorado Apples
1 cup raisins
½ cup chopped Bennett Pecans
2 tsp Rodelle Vanilla
maraschino cherries and pecan halves to decorate

- Cream sugar and butter; add beaten egg.
- Add mashed beans.
- Sift all remaining dry ingredients together; add to sugar mixture.
- Add apples, raisins, pecans and vanilla.
- Pour into well greased 10″ tube pan; bake in 375 degree oven 45 minutes.
- Remove from oven; cool before removing from pan.
- Decorate with maraschino cherries and pecan halves.
- Remove from oven; cool before removing from pan.
- Serves 16-20.

Lemon 7Up Cake

1 lemon cake mix
1 (6 oz) pkg lemon gelatin
2 cups boiling water
1 cup 7Up

Frosting:

1 (3.5 oz) pkg lemon instant pudding
1 cup Meadow Gold Milk
1 (8 oz) ctn whipped topping

- Prepare and bake cake mix according to pkg directions in 9″ x 13″ cake pan.
- While cake is baking, dissolve gelatin in boiling water; add 7Up.
- Remove cake from oven; poke holes in top with fork.
- Pour gelatin mixture over cake; refrigerate at least 4 hours.
- Mix instant pudding with milk; add whipped topping. Spread over cake.
- Serves 24-30.

BUYER'S GUIDE

Alcoholic Beverages/Brewing Products

Anheuser-Busch, Inc. (Budweiser, Busch, Bud Light, Michelob, Michelob Light, Dark and Dry, Natural Light, Dewey Stevens Master Cellars Wines, Asante), Fort Collins

Beich Company (Beich, Richlow), Denver

Boulder Brewing Company (Boulder Extra Pale Ale, Boulder Porter, Boulder Sport, Boulder Stout), Boulder

Carlson Vineyards (Carlson Vineyards), Palisade

Colorado Cellars (Colorado Cellars), Palisade

Coors Brewing Company (Coors, Coors Light and Extra Gold, Killian's Red, Keystone, Keystone Light, Winterfest), Golden

Hiram Walker Cordials and Liqueurs (Hiram Walker), Littleton

Kimoto Brewing Company (Kimoto), Boulder

Pikes Peak Vineyards (Pikes Peak Vineyards), Colorado Springs

Plum Creek Cellars, Ltd. (Plum Creek Cellars), Larkspur

Bakery Products

Ace Baking Company, Inc. (Ace), Denver

Agnes' Very, Very, Inc. (Agnes' Very, Very), Loveland

Bagel Bakery, The, Boulder

Batter Brilliance, Inc. (Batter Brilliance, Inc.), Aurora

Bennett Distributing Company, Denver

Bisetti's Cheesecake, Inc., Fort Collins

Bon Appetit (Gerard's), Denver

Booth Fisheries Company, Denver

Candy's Tortilla Factory, Inc., Pueblo

Continental Baking Company (Wonder Bread, Hostess, Home Pride), Denver

Creative Bakery, Boulder

Custom Blending, Inc., Fort Collins

Dolly Madison Bakery (Dolly Madison), Denver

Dough Bros. Inc., Cañon City

El Grande Food Processors (El Grande, Pablito's), Denver

Entemanns Inc./Oroweat Foods Company (Oroweat, Francisco, Star Deli), Denver

Fernandez Chile Co., Inc., Alamosa

Fiesta Products (Fiesta), Denver

Flite Services, Aurora

Fuller's Bakery, Fort Collins

Gargaro's Italian Bakery, Arvada

Home Style Bakery of Grand Junction, Inc., Grand Junction

Horizon Grain, Inc. (Horizon), Wray

Iron Pot Bakery, Inc., Denver

Ivanhoe Bakery, Inc., Arvada

Jan Holzmeister Cheesecake Ltd., Denver

Jose's of Brighton, Brighton

Keebler Company (Keebler), Denver

King Soopers Main Bakery, Denver

Kirchner's Bakery (Kirchner's), Colorado Springs

L & Z Tortilla, Inc., Brighton

La Popular Mexican Food Processors (La Popular), Denver

La Tolteca Foods, Inc. (La Tolteca), Pueblo

Le Francais Bakery, Boulder

Madonn's Cookies, Inc., Denver

Mama's Mexican Food Manufacturers, Inc. (Mama's), Colorado Springs

Mile-Hi Bakery, Denver

Mr. Bagel, Inc., Denver

Mrs. Hand's Cookies, Denver

Nabisco Brands, Inc. (Nabisco), Thornton

Old Fashioned Bavarian Bakery, Longmont

Our Name Is Mud, Inc., Denver

The Pletzel Corp., Denver

Pour La France! Bakery, Denver

Rainbo Bread Company (Rainbo), Denver

Ready Foods, Inc., Denver

Rios Tortillas Factory, Alamosa

Rockies Deli and Bakery, Denver

Rudi's Bakery, Boulder

Schmidt's Olde Time Bakery (Schmidt's), Loveland

Señor DeMecio's Tortilla Factory, Red Cliff

Shnooky's Cookies, Denver

Slice O Life Bakery, Palisade

Soloman Baking Co., Inc., Denver

Stehmans Wheat Products (Mr. Pancake), Greeley

Sunrise Pastries Corporation, Denver

Sweet Inspiration Dessert Company, Boulder

Verderaime Bakery, Pueblo

Vie De France Bakery Corporation (Vie de France), Denver

Candy, Nuts/Confectionery Products

Bass, R. H. Foods, Denver

Beich Company (Beich, Richlow), Denver

Bennett Distributing Company, Denver

Berthoud Candy Shoppe, Berthoud

Bremner Biscuit Company (Bremner), Denver

Chocolate Wanderbar, Lakewood

Dietrich's Chocolates, Denver

Enstrom Candies, Inc., Grand Junction

Food Products Co. (Mrs. Sutler's), Denver

Gram's Foods (Gram's), Golden

Half-Cracked Nut Co., Wheatridge

Hammond Candy Co., Inc., Denver

Jerry's Nut House, Inc. (Jerry's), Denver

Jolly Rancher Candies (Jolly Rancher), Wheat Ridge

Jon's Natural Bread, Fort Collins

Mountain Man Nut and Fruit Co., Parker

Naturally Nuts (Naturally Nuts), Boulder

Nouvelle Chocolat Inc./Topo Chocolate, Aurora

Nutorama "Little Nut House," Inc. (Little Nut House), Denver

Olathe Potato Growers Co-op Association, Olathe

Palisade Pride, Inc., Palisade

Patsy's Candies, Pride of the Rockies, Colorado Springs

Rocky Mountain Chocolate Factory (Rocky Mountain Chocolate Factory), Durango

Safeway Stores, Inc., Denver

Stephany's Chocolates, Denver

West's Finest Candy, The, Manitou Springs

Vern's Toffee House (Vern's), Fort Collins

Dairy Products

Anderson Boneless Beef, Inc. (Anderson's Pride), Denver

Anne and Mann's Gourmet Ice Cream, Colorado Springs

Bar-S Foods Co. (Bar-S, President's Pride), Phoenix, Arizona

Colorado City Creamery (Colorado City), Colorado Springs

Colorado Correctional Industries (Juniper Valley Farms), Colorado Springs

Colorado Frozen Yogurt, Inc., Englewood

Dreyer's Grand Ice Cream (Dreyer's Grand Ice Cream), Denver

Eckert Creamery, Inc. (Challenge, Rocky Mountain), Eckert

Golden Peaks Dairy (Golden Peaks), Golden

Graves & Graves (Graves Dairy), Bellvue

Harper Dairy, Yuma

Hertzke Holsteins, Greeley

Jackson Ice Cream Company, Inc., Denver

K-Mac Yogurt, Inc., Denver

Lakes, Inc. (Lakes), Denver

Leprino Foods Company (Leprino), Denver

Lickety Split Ice Cream (Lickety Split), Denver

Lowell-Paul Dairy, Inc., Greeley

Magills World of Ice Cream, Lakewood

Meadow Gold Dairies (Viva, Olde Style, Meadow Gold, Holland, Louis Sherry), Englewood
Mountain High Yoghurt (Mountain High), Englewood
Robinson Dairy (Robinson, Bonjour), Denver
Royal Crest Dairy (Royal Crest), Denver
Safeway Stores, Inc., Denver
Scanga Meat Company, Salida
Schreiber Foods, Inc. (Schreiber), Aurora
Sinton Food Companies, Inc., Colorado Springs
Stephany's Chocolates, Denver
Tofruzen, Inc., Englewood
Western Dairymen Cooperative, Inc. (Cream O'Weber, Hi-Land, Challenge, Cache Valley, Twin Falls), Thorton
White Wave, Inc. (White Wave, Soy Foods Unlimited), Boulder
Zubal Goat Dairy, Hoehne

Flour/Other Grain Mill Products

Adobe Milling Company, Inc. (Adobe Milling), Dove Creek
Alfa-Flour, Inc., Wray
Best of Colorado, The/C-Bar (C-Bar), Aurora
Brewbakers, Denver
C. B. Enterprises, Inc., Bloomfield
Colorado Cereal, Inc., Yuma
Conagra Flour Milling Company (Hungarian Flour), Commerce City
El Molino Foods (El Molino, LaFamous), Denver
Griffin-Holder Company (Sombrero, Solar), Rocky Ford
Hall Grain Company, Akron
Henderson Mills (Eartharvest), Fort Morgan
High Country Elevator, Dove Creek
Horizon Grain, Inc. (Horizon), Wray
Mady's Specialty Foods (Mady's), Aurora
Mountain Maid (Mountain Maid), Center
Mt Mama Mills/Gosar Ranch (Mt Mama Flour), Monte Vista
Nabisco Brands, Inc. (Nabisco), Denver
Nicol Agri-Services, Hoehne
Otis Milling Company/Wheat Land Farms (Wheat Land Farms), Yuma
Paoli Farmers Cooperative Elevator Company, Paoli
Stehmans Wheat Products (Mr. Pancake), Greeley

Fresh Fruits/Melons

Apple Hill Orchards Juice Company, Dolores
Bellwether Farms (Bellwether Farms), Fort Collins
C. B. C. Colorado Berry Company, Austin
Cedaredge Fruitgrowers, Inc. (Thunder Mountain), Cedaredge
Colorado Correctional Industries (Juniper Valley Farms), Colorado Springs
Colorado Mountain Vineyards (Colorado Mountain Vineyards), Palisade
Federal Fruit and Produce Co., Denver
Gobbo Farms and Orchards (Go For Go-Bo), Grand Junction
Golden West Farms (Golden West), Brighton
Griffin-Holder Company (Sombrero, Solar), Rocky Ford
Hi-Quality Packing, Inc. (Tom Tom Wigwam), Delta
Honeyville (Honeyville, Mountain Bouquet), Durango
Lusk Produce Company, Rocky Ford
McPherson Orchards (McPherson Orchards), Cedaredge
Mesa Foods, Loveland
Our Name Is Mud, Inc., Denver
Palisade Pride, Inc., Palisade
Piedmont Farms, Inc. (Grant Farms, Colorado's Finest, Piedmont Farms), Wellington
P & M Fruit Company (P & M), Eckert
Pikes Peak Vineyards (Pikes Peak Vineyards), Colorado Springs
Plum Creek Cellars, Ltd. (Plum Creek Cellars), Larkspur
Rocky Ford Produce Company (Rocky Ford, Pride of Rocky Ford), Rocky Ford
Rogers Mesa Fruit Co. (Silver Spruce), Hotchkiss
Sisson Orchards, Palisade

Summit Farms, Inc., Center
Sweetheart Farms (Sweetheart Farms), Berthoud
Talbott Farms, Inc. (Talbott Farms) Palisade
Thomas Produce and Farms, Pueblo
United Fruit Growers Association, Palisade
United Fruit Packing, Inc. (Thunderbold, Surface Creek Orchards), Austin
William D. Grasmick, Inc., Granda
Wilson's Hi-Country Fruit (Hi-Country), Paonia

Fresh Vegetables

Adobe Milling Company, Inc. (Anasazi Brothers), Dove Creek
Agronix, Inc., La Junta
Alpine Potato Company, Hooper
Arkansas Valley Produce (A-V), Wiley
Bass, R. H., Foods, Denver
Bellwether Farms (Inch By Inch), Fort Collins
Blanfort, Inc. (Hi-Dolly), Blanca
Bliss Produce Company, Greeley
Campion Greenhouses (Campion Greenhouses), Loveland
Cañon Potato Company (Cañon, Capco, Lede, Jim Jo), Center
Charley Hayashida Farms, Inc. (Charley Hayashida), Blanca
Colorado Potato Growers' Exchange, Denver
Delta Potato Growers Cooperative Association (Sunny West), Delta
Domenico Farms, Denver
Elliott Gardens, Denver
Ellithorpe & Son, Center
Entz Farms, Center
Fagerberg, Kenny, Produce, Ault
Federal Fruit and Produce Co., Denver
Grasmick, William D., Inc., Granada
Gobbo Farms and Orchards (Go For Go-Bo), Grand Junction
Golden West Farms (Golden West Farms), Brighton
Griffin-Holder Company (Sombrero, Solar), Rocky Ford
Grower Shipper Potato Company (Growers Pride, Colorado Gold, Pay Day), Monte Vista
Harold Tateyama & Sons, Inc. (Tateys), Ault
Hi-Land Potato Company (Hi-Land), Monte Vista
Hines Farms, Inc., Delta
Hungenberg Produce Company (Crispac), Greeley
Hydro-Gardens, Inc. (Chem-Gro), Colorado Springs
Life Force Foods (Life Force), Boulder
Lusk Produce Company, Rocky Ford
Marshall Produce Company, Monte Vista
Martin Produce Company (Martin's Leader, Hoyles Best), Greeley
Metz Potato Company, Monte Vista
Milliken Early Potato Association, Gilcrest
Monson Brothers Company, Greeley
Montrose Potato Growers (Colorancho Onions, Outwest Pinto Beans, Western Seed), Montrose
Mrs. Condies Salad Company, Inc. (Condies), Denver
North Weld Produce Company, Greeley
Olathe Potato Growers Co-Op Association, Olathe
Onion Growers, Inc. (Sun Tan, OGI, Banner, Welco, Premium) Ault
Papst Robbins Company (Farm Fresh), Denver
Piedmont Farms, Inc. (Grant Farms), Wellington
Rakhra Mushroom Farm Corporation (Rakhra), Alamosa
Rocky Ford Produce Company (Rocky Ford), Rocky Ford
Rosey Farms (Rosey Farms), Ignacio
Sakata Farms, Inc., Brighton
Sam's Produce, Inc. (Sam's Produce, Top Quality), Denver
Sisson Orchards, Palisade
Springs Gardens, Inc., Rifle
Summit Farms, Inc., Center
Tanaka Farms, Erie
Thomas Produce and Farms, Pueblo
Thompson Potato Company, LaSalle
Tuxedo Corn Co., Olathe

United Fruit Growers Association, Palisade
Vertical Integrated Processing, Greeley
Villano Brothers, Fort Lupton
Wilsons' High Country Fruit, Paonia
Wolf Creek Potato Company (Centennial, Russet Burbank, Red McClure), Monte Vista
Wright Brothers, Inc. (Blue Goose), Monte Vista

Fruits/Vegetables, Frozen

Bevco 2 Industries Corporation, Denver
Booth Fisheries Company, Denver
City Ice Company (City Ice, Party Pride, Tour National, Espy Ice), Denver
Food City U.S.A., Inc. (Grandma's Frozen Pies), Denver
Frozen Foods, Inc. (FFI), Rocky Ford
Gelato Bravo!, Littleton
Gram's Foods (Gram's), Golden
Kirchner's Bakery (Kirchner's), Colorado Springs
Magills World of Ice Cream (Magills), Lakewood
Mesa Foods (Mesa), Loveland
Orange Juice Daily, Inc., Denver
Ready Foods, Inc., Denver
Ready Ice Company, Cañon City
Silver State Foods (Salvatore's & Aiello's Italian Foods), Denver
Shnooky's Cookies, Denver
Tico's Mexican Foods (Tico's), Denver
Tour Ice of Durango, Inc., Durango
White Wave, Inc. (White Wave, Tofruzen, Soyfoods Unlimited), Boulder

Fruits/Vegetables, Pickled, etc.

Flite Services, Aurora
Gram's Foods (Gram's), Golden
Green Bay Food Company, Inc., La Junta
Jensen's Blue Ribbon Processing (Jensen's), Fowler
Kennedy Foods, Inc., Denver
Nona Morelli (Nona Morelli), Pueblo West
Palisade Pride, Inc. (Palisade Pride), Palisade
St. Mary's Gourmet Foods., Inc. (St. Mary's), Denver
Tico's Mexican Foods (Tico's), Denver

Fruits/Vegetables, Processed

All American Seasonings, Inc. (All American Seasonings) Denver
Apple Hill Orchards (Mountain Sun, Apple Hill Orchards), Delores
Bass, R. H., Foods, Denver
Beich Company (Beich, Richlow), Denver
Bliss Produce Company, Greeley
Bennett Distributing Company, Denver
Chapin's Supreme Foods (Chapin's Supreme), Denver
Colorado Spice Company, The (Colorado Spice Company), Denver
Creative Crafts Corporation (Gramp's Farm), Fruita
Custom Blending, Inc. (Nate's, Rodelle), Fort Collins
Diven Packing Co (Diven, Kuner's, Mile High, Cream of the Valley), Fowler
Flite Services, Aurora
Fowler Co-Operative Association, Fowler
Fort Lupton Canning Company, Fort Lupton
Fresh Colorado Squeezed, Littleton
Green Bay Food Company, Inc., La Junta
Just Squeezed Juices (Just Squeezed Juices), Denver
Kennedy Foods, Inc., Denver
Lakes, Inc. (Lakes), Denver
Leroux Creek Food Corp. (Palisade Pride), Hotchkiss
Marquest (Marquest), Erie
Merlino, Inc. (Merlinos Cider Company), Cañon City
Mesa Foods (Mesa), Loveland
Mountain Sun Organic & Natural Juices (Mountain Sun), Delores
Orange Juice Daily, Inc., Denver
Palisade Pride, Inc., (Palisade Pride, Inc.), Hotchkiss
Rainbow Juices, Boulder
Robinson Dairy, Inc. (Robinson, Bonjour), Denver

Silver State Foods (Aiello's), Denver
St. Mary's Gourmet (St. Mary's), Denver
Stokes-Ellis Foods Company (Stokes, Ellis), Denver
Tico's Mexican Foods (Tico's), Denver
Whitehouse-Skyland Food Corporation (Skyland), Delta

Grain - Grains/Beans, Food

Adobe Milling Company, Inc. (Adobe Milling, Anasazi Beans), Dove Creek
Agate Elevator, Agate
Agland, Inc. (Redbird Brand), Eaton
Agtec, Inc., Flagler
Alfa-Flour, Inc., Wray
Allen Grain, Inc., Idalia
Amherst Cooperative Elevator, Inc., Amherst
Amity Milling Company, Holly
Arriba Grain, Inc., Arriba
Audubon Park Company, Akron
Awful John's Grain Exchange, Inc., Deer Trail
Bennett Distributing Company, Denver
Berger and Company, Greeley
Best of Colorado/C-Bar, Aurora
Boone Bean & Elevator Company, Boone
Carhart Feed & Seed, Dove Creek
Centennial Commodities, Inc., Denver
Cheyenne Farmers Elevator Company, Inc., Cheyenne Wells
Colorado Agri-Feed, Inc., Colorado Springs
Colorado Beef, Lamar
Colorado Cereal, Inc. (Colorado Cereal, Inc.), Yuma
Colorado Potato Growers' Exchange, Denver
Colorado-Kansas Grain Company (Lamar, Carlton, Burlington, Idalia, Colorado-Kansas Grain Company), Lamar
Coors Brewing Company, Golden
Cox Grain Company, Inc., Brush
Delta Potato Growers Cooperative Association (SunnyWest, Golden Beauty), Delta
Dorsch Grain & Mfg. (Dorsch Grain & Mfg.), Flagler
Dracon Grain Company, Julesburg
Eads Consumers Supply Company, Inc. (Haswell Elevator), Haswell
Excello Commodities, Inc., Denver
Farmers Cooperative Elevator Company, Fleming
Farmers Elevator Company (Colorado's Finest Pinto Beans), Ovid
Farmers Marketing Association, Denver
Farmers Union Co-Operative Elevator Company, Wray
Flagler Equity Co-Operative Company, Flagler
Food Products Company (Mrs. Sutler's), Denver
Fowler Co-operative Association, Fowler
Gingerbear House, Inc., The (The Gingerbear House), Lakewood
Gobbo Farms and Orchards (Go for Go-Bo, Piñon Mesa), Grand Junction
Goodman Grain & Seed Company, Akron
Grasmick, William D., Granada
Griffin-Holder Company (Sombrero, Solar), Rocky Ford
Hall Grain Company, Akron
Harper Dairy, Yuma
Henderson Mills, Fort Morgan
Hi-Land Potato Company (Hi-Land), Monte Vista
High Country Elevator, Dove Creek
High Summit Foods (Foster's), Denver
Hillary Mills (Popt Wheat), Fort Collins
Hines Farms, Inc., Delta
Holly Farms, Inc., Holly
Horizon Grain, Inc. (Horizon), Wray
Howard's of Colorado, Boulder
Jack's Bean Company, Fort Morgan
Johnstown Feed & Seed, Inc., Johnstown
Lousberg Grain & Feed, Sterling
Loveland Feed & Grain Company, Loveland
M. J. K. Sales & Feed, Inc., Craig
Manna Pro Country (Manna Pro), Colorado Springs
McKenzie Farms (Tiegra Negra Farms), Boulder

Metz Potato Company, Monte Vista
Mitie Mixes, Inc. (Mitie Mixes), Fort Collins
Monte Vista Co-Op, Monte Vista
Montrose Potato Growers (Colorancho Onions, Outwest Pinto Beans, Western Seed), Montrose
Mountain Maid (Mountain Maid), Center
Mt Mama Mills/Gosar (Mt Mama Flour), Monte Vista
Mountain States Bean Company, Inc. (Pantry), Denver
Nicol Agri-Services, Hoehne
North Weld Produce Company, Greeley
October Mountain Charolais, Las Animas
Olathe Potato Growers Co-Op Association (Hub of the Uncompahgre Cowboy), Olathe
Paoli Farmers Cooperative Elevator Company, Paoli
Peetz Farmers Co-Operative Company, Peetz
Perry Brothers Seed, Inc., Otis
Piedmont Farms, Inc. (Grant Farms), Wellington
Ralph Conrad, Flagler
Reuben Bostron Farms, Inc., Fort Morgan
Red Beard Bean (Red Beard Bean), Delta
Rocky Ford Produce Company (Rocky Ford, Pride of Rocky Ford), Rocky Ford
Roggen Farmers Elevator Association, Roggen
Scoular Grain Company, Monte Vista
Showalter Agricultural Center, Inc., Swink
Snell Grain & Feed, Inc., Hugo
Snell Grain of Arriba, Inc., Arriba
Snell Grain of Genoa, Inc., Genoa
Snyder & Counts Feed, Craig
Southwest Colorado Bean Producers, Inc., Yellow Jacket
Springfield Cooperative Sales Company, Springfield
Stratton Equity Cooperative Company, Stratton
Summit Farms, Inc., Center
Sunshine Industries, Yellow Jacket
Sweeny Feed Mill of South Colorado, Inc., Pueblo
Sweetheart Farms (Sweetheart Farms), Berthoud
Tempel & Esgar, Inc., Wiley
Thomas Produce and Farms, Pueblo
Thunder Mountain Bean Company, Delta
Trinidad/Benham Corporation (Benco-Peak, Evans, Diamond, Ranch Wagon, Cook Quick, Triad), Denver
United Farmers Marketing Corp. (People's Choice), Burlington
United Grain Corporation of Colorado, Cheyenne Wells
Valley Mill & Feed Company, Wiley
Western International Grain Company, Aurora
Wheat Land Farms (Wheat Land Farms), Yuma
Wiggins Farmers Co-Op Elevator, Wiggins
Wray Grain Company, Wray
Yuma County Grain Company, Inc., Yuma

Jams/Jellies/Preserves

Apple Hill Orchards (Mountain Sun, Apple Hill Orchards), Delores
Fowler Co-Operative Association, Fowler
Gingerbear House, Inc., The (The Gingerbear House), Lakewood
Gramp's Farm, Fruita
Green Bay Food Company, Inc., La Junta
Honeyville (Honeyville, Mountain Bouquet), Durango
Mady's Specialty Foods (Mady's), Aurora
Merlino, Inc. (Merlinos Cider Company), Cañon City
Mountain Maid (Mountain Maid), Center
Palisade Pride, Inc. (Palisade Pride, Inc.), Palisade
Rainbow Juices, Boulder
Robinson Dairy, Inc. (Robinson, Bonjour), Denver
Rocky Mountain Natural Foods (Rocky Mountain Natural Foods), Crested Butte
Skyland Food Corporation (Skyland), Delta
Stokes-Ellis Foods Company, Denver
Tico's Mexican Foods (Tico's), Denver

Meat/Meat By-Products

Beef
Anderson Boneless Beef, Inc. (Anderson's Pride), Denver

Banes Custom Pack (Banes), Cortez
Bar-S Foods Co. (Bar-S, President's Pride), Phoenix, Arizona
Best of Colorado/C-Bar, Aurora
Booth Fisheries Company, Denver
Brush Locker System, Brush
Callaway Packing Inc., Delta
Cedaredge Meats, Inc. (Cedaredge), Cedaredge
Champion Boxed Beef, Denver
Coleman Natural Meats, Inc. (Coleman Natural Meats), Denver
Colorado Beef, Lamar
Colorado Beef Company, Delta
Columbine Meat Packing, Inc., Denver
Crystal Springs Ranch & Trout Farm, Hotchkiss
D & L Meat Company, Ovid
Denver Boneless Beef Company, Denver
Donnelly Ranch/Mesa De Maya Natural Beef (Mesa De Maya Natural Beef), Kim
El Grande Food Processors (El Grande, Pablito's), Denver
Elizabeth Locker Plant, Elizabeth
Excel Corporation, Englewood
European Sausage Company (European Sausage Company), Castle Rock
F & R Meat Company Inc., Denver
G & C Packing Company, Colorado Springs
Galligan Wholesale Meat Company, Inc., Denver
Gold Star Sausage Company Inc., Denver
Graves & Graves (Grave's Dairy, Pleasant Valley Beef, Litter Green), Bellvue
Hotchkiss Meats, Hotchkiss
House of Smoke, Inc., Fort Lupton
I. F. P. Company, Denver
Lombardi Brothers Meat Packers, Inc., Denver
Loveland Foods/Continental Grain Company (Old Time Meat Products), Loveland
Lowrey's Meat Specialties, Inc. (Lowrey's, Bighorn), Denver
Maverick Ranch Lite Beef, Inc. (NaturaLite Beef), Denver
Miniat, Ed, Inc., Englewood
Monfort of Colorado, Inc. (Monfort, Inc.), Greeley
Monfort Portion Foods, Greeley
Monroe's Economy Meat & Lockers, Arvada
Mountain City Meats, Denver
Nicol Agri-Services, Hoehne
O'Connor Meat Company, Inc., Littleton
Old World Meat Company, Grand Junction
Pepcol Manufacturing Company, Denver
Petrie Meat Processing, Pierce
Quality Meat Company (Nugget, Quality Meat), Grand Junction
Quality Packing Inc., Sterling
Rocky Mountain Meats, Denver
Scanga Meat Company, Salida
Sigman Meat Company (Top Dog, Gold Nugget, Mile High), Arvada
Sterling By-Products, Sterling
Sterling Beef, Englewood
Supervised Products, Commerce City
Temptee Brand Steak, Inc. (Temptee Specialty Foods), Arvada
Valley Packing Inc., La Salle
Weld County Bi-Products, Greeley

Fish
Anderson Boneless Beef, Inc. (Anderson's Pride), Denver
Aquafarm Associates of Colorado, Inc. (Colorado Mountain Bass), Denver
Artic Pacific Fisheries, Denver
Booth Fisheries Company, Denver
Bovee's Trout Ranch, Salida
Cline Trout Farms, Boulder
Crystal Springs Ranch & Trout Farm, Hotchkiss
Dowling Enterprises, Inc. (Dowling's), Denver
Four Seasons Trout Farm, Cedaredge
H & H Hatchery, Creede

Hagen Western Fisheries, Inc. (Colorado Rainbow Brand), Fort Collins
Keeton Fisheries Consultants, Inc., Fort Collins
Krabloonik Country Meat & Specialty Co., El Jebel
Rainbow Falls Park & Fish Hatchers, Woodland
Rainbow Springs Trout Ranch, Durango
Rio Grande Trout Hatchery, Creede
Silver Springs Trout Farm, Montrose
Smoke Ranch Ltd., Denver
Sweeny Feed Mill of South Colorado, Inc., Pueblo
Twin Buttes Trout Ranch, Durango
Queen of the River Fish Company, Inc., Longmont

Lamb

Anderson Boneless Beef (Anderson's Pride), Denver
Banes Custom Pack, Cortez
Brush Locker System, Inc., Brush
Callaway Packing, Inc. (Callaway), Delta
Cedaredge Meats, Inc. (Cedaredge), Cedaredge
Coleman Natural Beef (Coleman Alpine Lamb), Denver
Colorado Lamb Company (Colorado Lamb), Denver
Denver Lamb Company, Denver
Elizabeth Locker Plant, Elizabeth
Galligan Wholesale Meat Company, Inc., Denver
Hotchkiss Meats, Hotchkiss
Lombardi Brothers Meat Packers, Inc., Denver
Monfort of Colorado, Inc., Greeley
Monfort Portion Foods, Greeley
Monroe's Economy Market & Lockers, Arvada
Mountain Meadows Lamb Corporation (Mountain Meadows Lamb), Denver
Nicol Agri-Services, Hoehne
Petrie Meat Processing, Pierce
Quality Meat Company (Quality Meat), Grand Junction
Quality Packing, Inc., Sterling
Rocky Mountain Meats, Denver
Scanga Meat Company, Salida
Valley Packing, Inc., La Salle
Weld County Bi-Products, Greeley

Pork

Anderson Boneless Beef, Inc. (Anderson's Pride), Denver
Banes Custom Pack, Cortez
Bar-S Foods Co. (Bar-S, President's Pride), Phoenix, AZ
Booth Fisheries Company, Denver
Brush Locker System, Brush
Callaway Packing Inc. (Callaway), Delta
Canino's (Canino's), Denver
Cedaredge Meats, Inc. (Cedaredge), Cedaredge
Clyde's Italian and German Sausage, Inc., Denver
Continental Sausage (Mr. Green Sausage), Longmont
Decker & Son (Pig in the Sack), Colorado Springs
El Grande Food Processors (El Grande, Pablito's), Denver
Elizabeth Locker Plant, Inc., Elizabeth
European Meat Products, Inc. (European Sausage), Lakewood
European Sausage Company, Castle Rock
Galligan Wholesale Meat Company, Inc., Denver
Gold Star Sausage Company, Inc., Denver
Hickory Baked Ham Co., Littleton
Hotchkiss Meats, Hotchkiss
House of Smoke, Inc. (House of Smoke), Fort Lupton
Jensen's Blue Ribbon Processing (Jensen's), Fowler
L & Z Tortilla, Inc.
Lombardi Brothers Meat Packers, Inc., Denver
Loveland Foods/Continental Grain Company, Loveland
Monfort Portion Foods, Greeley
Monroe's Economy Market & Lockers, Arvada
Mt Mama Mills/Gosar Ranch (Gosar Barvarian Sausage), Monte Vista
Mountain Man Sausage Co., Inc., Englewood
Old West Sausage Co. (Old West Sausage), Longmont
Old World Meat Company, Grand Junction
Ostermann Sausage Company, Denver
Petrie Meat Processing, Pierce

Quality Meat Company, Inc. (Nugget, Quality Meat), Grand Junction
Quality Packing, Inc., Sterling
Randy's Frozen Steaks, Inc., Arvada
Rocky Mountain Meats, Denver
Sara's Sausage, Palmer Lake
Scanga Meat Company, Salida
Schreiber Foods, Inc., Aurora
Sigman Meat Company (Top Dog, Gold Nugget, Mile High), Arvada
Sisneros Brothers Packing Company, Inc., Pueblo
Valley Packing, Inc., La Salle

Poultry/Eggs

Anderson Boneless Beef, Inc. (Anderson's Pride), Denver
Banes Custom Pack (Banes), Cortez
Barber's Poultry, Inc. (Barber's), Bloomfield
Booth Fisheries Company, Denver
Brush Locker System, Inc., Brush
Callaway Packing, Inc. (Callaway), Delta
Canino's (Canino's), Denver
Colorado Poultry, Denver
Elizabeth Locker Plant, Inc., Elizabeth
Galligan Wholesale Meat Company, Inc., Denver
Hall's Duck Technology, Inc., Las Animas
I. F. P. Company, Denver
Kashiwa Teriyaki, Inc. (Kashiwa), Boulder
Lombardi Brothers Meat Packers, Inc., Denver
Longmont Foods Company (Longmont, Lite Supreme), Longmont
Milton G. Waldbaum Company, Hudson
Scanga Meat Company, Salida

Processed Meat/Game

Anderson Boneless Beef (Anderson's Pride), Denver
Bar-S Foods Co. (Bar-S, President's Pride), Phoenix, Arizona Brush Locker System, Brush
Championship Recipe Foods (Championship Recipe), Boulder
Colorado Jerkey Company, Westminster
Custom Blending, Inc., Fort Collins
Custom Corned Beef, Inc. (Custom Corned Beef), Denver
Daddy Bruce's Bar-B-Que, Denver
Dale's Exotic Game Meats, Denver
European Meat Products, Inc., Lakewood
Four Corners Rabbit (Four Corners), Durango
Hotchkiss Meats, Hotchkiss
House of Smoke, Inc. (House of Smoke), Fort Lupton
I. F. P. Company, Denver
Kaatz Gourmet Co., Inc., Evergreen
Krabloonik Country Meat & Specialty Co., El Jabel
Lay Valley Bison Ranch, Craig
Lombardi Brothers Meat Packers, Inc., Denver
Meadow Buffalo, Inc., Denver
Quality Meat Company, Inc. (Quality Meat), Grand Junction
Quality Packing, Inc., Sterling
Red Bird Farms, Co., Littleton
Rocky Mountain Natural Meats, Denver
Sisneros Brothers Packing Company, Inc., Pueblo
Sterling By-Products, Inc., Sterling
Valley Packing, Inc., La Salle
Weld County Bi-Products, Greeley
Wyman Elk Ranch, Craig

Nationality/Specialty Foods

Amigo's Tortilla Factory, Denver
Batter Brilliance, Inc. (Batter Brilliance, Inc.), Aurora
Bear Creek Apiaries (High Country Honey), Morrison
Best of Colorado/C-Bar, Aurora
Blue Parrot, Inc., Louisville
Cajun Foods West, Inc. (Larry Price), Louisville
Candy's Tortilla Factory, Inc., Pueblo
China Dragon Gourmet Enterprises, Inc. (China Dragon), Fort Collins
D & L Meat Company, Ovid

Denver To-Fu Company (Denver To-Fu), Denver
Dowling Enterprises, Inc. (Dowling's), Denver
Dough Bros. Inc., Cañon City
El Grande Food Processors (El Grande, Pablito's), Denver
European Meat Products, Inc., Lakewood
Fernandez Chile Co., Inc., Alamosa
Fiesta Products (Fiesta), Denver
Frangi's Italian Foods, Inc. (Frangi's), Denver
Great Western Tortilla Company, The (Dos Hombres, GW), Denver
Greens and Powder, Colorado Springs
High Country Foods, Inc. (Early Bird), Denver
High Summit Foods Company (Little Chalet, Peak Peppers, Serious Salsa), Denver
House of Smoke, Inc. (House of Smoke), Fort Lupton
Jose's of Brighton, Brighton
Kashiwa Teriyaki, Inc. (Kashiwa), Boulder
Kennedy Foods, Inc., Denver
L & Z Tortilla, Inc., Brighton
La Favorita, Denver
Lala's Mexican Deli, Denver
La Tolteca Foods, Inc. (La Tolteca), Pueblo
Mady's Specialty Foods (Mady's), Denver
Mama's Mexican Food Manufacturers, Inc. (Mama's), Colorado Springs
Morelli, Nona (Nona Morelli), Pueblo West
Pasta Via International (Pasta Via), Evergreen
Quality Packing, Inc., Sterling
Ready Foods, Inc., Denver
Rios Tortillas Factory, Alamosa
Silver State Foods (Salvatore's & Aiello's Italian Foods), Denver
Scaff Brothers (F & J Brand), La Junta
Señor DeMecio's Tortilla Factory, Red Cliff
Sequoyah Foods (Sequoyah), Denver
St. Mary's Gourmet Foods, Inc. (St. Mary's), Denver
Stokes-Ellis Foods Company (Stokes, Ellis), Denver
Tamale Factory, Colorado Springs
Great Western Tortilla Company, The (Great Western, Mi Ranchita), Denver
Tico's Mexican Foods (Tico's), Denver
White Wave, Inc. (White Wave), Boulder

Pasta

Bennett Distributing Company, Denver
Boyer Coffee Company (Pastarific), Denver
Denver To-Fu Company (Denver To-Fu), Denver
Food City U.S.A., Inc. (Grandma's Frozen Pasta), Denver
Frangi's Italian Foods, Inc. (Frangi's), Denver
Nona Morelli (Nona Morelli) Pueblo West
Pasta Pasta Pasta (Pasta Pasta Pasta), Denver
Pasta Via International, Evergreen
Scanga Meat Company, Salida
Silver State Foods (Salvatore's), Denver

Shortening/Other Edible Fats/Oils

Anderson Boneless Beef, Inc. (Anderson's Pride), Denver
Brown's Food Products (Lakes), Denver
Loveland Foods Continental Grain Company, Loveland
Pepcol Manufacturing Company, Denver

Sauces/Seasonings/Spices/Mustards/Salad Dressings

All American Seasonings, Inc. (All American Seasonings), Denver
Appalachian Specialties, Ltd. (Judges Choice), Aurora
Beich Company (Beich, Richlow), Denver
Blue Parrot, Inc., Louisville
Cajun Foods West, Inc. (Larry Price's), Louisville
Championship Recipe Foods (Championship Recipe), Boulder
Chapin's Supreme Foods (Chapin's Supreme), Denver
China Dragon Gourmet Enterprises, Inc. (China Dragon), Fort Collins
Colorado Spice Company, The (The Colorado Spice Company), Denver

Creative Crafts Corporation (Gramp's Farm), Fruita
Custom Blending, Inc. (Nate's, Rodelle), Fort Collins
Dixon & Sons Barbeque Sauce, Inc. (Dixon & Sons), Aurora
Elliott Gardens, Denver
Fernandez Chile Co., Inc., Alamosa
Frangi's Italian Foods, Inc. (Frangi), Denver
Gingerbear House, Inc., The (The Gingerbear House), Lakewood
Greens and Powder, Colorado Springs
Herbs of China, Ltd., Boulder
High Summit Foods Company (Little Chalet, Peak Peppers, Serious Salsa, Chavez Chili, Foster's), Denver
Hot Roxx, Aurora
Lucile's Creole Food Products (Lucile's Creole Seasonings, Lucile's New Orleans Style Coffees), Boulder
Kashiwa Teriyaki, Inc. (Kashiwa), Denver
Kennedy Foods, Inc., Denver
M & H Foods, Inc., Fort Collins
Mady's Specialty Foods (Mady's), Aurora
More Than Mustard (More Than Mustard), Denver
Old Savannah Company, Inc., Aurora
Pasta Via International, Evergreen
Pierre's Food Products, Denver
Rava Foods (Rosalie's), Brush
Ready Foods, Inc., Denver
Scaff Brothers (F & J Brand), La Junta
Sequoyah Foods (Sequoyah Foods), Denver
Specialty Spices, Niwot
St. Mary's Gourmet Foods, Inc. (St. Mary's), Denver
Taylor's Premium Sauces/Windward Corp., Boulder
White Wave, Inc. (White Wave, Soyfoods Unlimited), Boulder

Sugar/Honey

Ambrosia Honey Company (Ambrosia Honey), Parachute
Bear Creek Apiaries (High Country Honey), Morrison
Beich Company (Beich, Richlow), Denver
C. B. Enterprises, Inc., Bloomfield
Caldwell Honey Company, Debeque
Colorado City Creamery (Colorado City Creamery), Colorado Springs
Colorado Sunshine Honey Co., Englewood
Columbine Beverage Company, Denver
Coors Biotech Products Company, Boulder
Duffy Products Company (Duffy, Royal Best, Nature Sweet), Denver
Graham's Golden Honey, Fowler
High Country Honey, Morrison
Hind's Honey Farms, La Jara
Holly Sugar Corporation (Holly), Colorado Springs
Honeyville (Honeyville), Durango
Kimoto Brewing Company (Kimoto), Boulder
Lakes, Inc. (Lakes), Denver
Madhava Honey Ltd. (Colorado Clover, Western Wildflower), Longmont
Niwot Honey Farm, Niwot
Rice's Lucky Clover (Lucky Clover, Frosty Acres), Greeley
Western Sugar Company, The (GW), Denver

Tea/Snacks/Beverages/Health Foods

Alfa-Flour, Inc., Wray
Allegro Coffee Company (Allegro Fine Coffee, Gold Label), Boulder
Aspen Mineral Water Company, Boulder
Bass, R. H., Foods, Denver
Bee Bee Que, Commerce City
Bennett Distributing Company, Denver
Berger and Company, Greeley
Best of Colorado, The/C-Bar, Aurora
Bevco 2 Industries Corporation, Denver
Bliss Produce Company, Greeley
Boyer Coffee Company (Boyer's), Denver

Bremner Biscuit Company, Denver
Candy's Tortilla Factory, Inc. (Candy's), Pueblo
Celestial Seasonings (Celestial Seasonings), Boulder
City Ice Company (City Ice, Party Pride, Tour National),
  Denver
Colorado Poppin Gold (Colorado Poppin Gold), Littleton
Columbine Beverage Company, Denver
Country Crisp Foods, Westminster
Custom Blending, Inc. (Nate's, Rodelle), Fort Collins
Deep Rock Water Company (Deep Rock), Denver
Denver Coca-Cola Bottling Company (Coca-Cola Classic,
  Coke, Sprite, Tab), Denver
Denver To-Fu Company (Denver To-Fu), Denver
Duffy Products Company (Duffy, Royal Best, Nature
  Sweet), Denver
Earth Dance Foods (Earth Dance), Fort Collins
Fiesta Products (Fiesta), Denver
Food Products Company (Mrs. Sutler's), Denver
Frito-Lay, Inc. (Lay's, Ruffles, Doritos, Tostitos), Denver
Full Service Beverage Company of Colorado (7Up, RC
  Cola, Canada Dry, Crush, Sunkist, Hawaiian Punch),
  Englewood
General Tea Corporation, Denver
Gourmet Kernels (Singer Foods), Aurora
Great Western Tortilla Co. (Dos Hombres, GW), Denver
High Country Foods, Inc. (Early Bird), Denver
Hillary Mills (Popt Wheat), Fort Collins
J. B.'s Corn 'N Yogurt (J. B.'s) Fort Collins
Jerry's Nut House, Inc. (Jerry's), Denver
L & Z Tortilla, Inc., Brighton
Lane Sales, Inc./Pepsi Cola Bottling Company (Squirt,
  Allied Brands, A & W), Colorado Springs
La Popular Mexican Food Processors (La Popular),
  Denver
La Tolteca Foods, Inc. (La Tolteca, Mexican Bear), Pueblo
Lowrey's Meat Specialties, Inc. (Lowrey's, Bighorn),
  Denver
Mady's Specialty Foods (Mady's), Aurora
Manna Pro Country Stores (Manna Pro), Colorado Springs
Meadow Buffalo, Inc., Denver
Mountain States Bean Company, Inc. (Pantry), Denver
Nabisco Brands, Inc. (Nabisco), Thornton
Naturally Nuts Company (Naturally Nuts), Boulder
Nicol Agri-Services, Hoehne
Olathe Potato Growers Co-Op Association, Olathe
Pigout Popcorn, Golden
Pletzel Corp., The, Denver
Rainbow Juices, Boulder
Ready Ice Company, Cañon City
Red Seal Snack Company (Red Seal, Barrel O'Fun,
  Kruncher's, El Dorado, Bravo, Laura Scudder, Little
  Pancho), Denver
Reuben Bostron Farms, Inc. (Bostron Farms),
  Fort Morgan
Rich Brothers, Boulder
Roberts Snacks, Inc. (Roberts), Broomfield
Rocky Mountain Beverage Company (Colorado Crystal),
  Denver
Rocky Mountain Natural Foods, Crested Butte
Rocky Mountain Popcorn Factory, Denver
Safeway Stores, Inc., Denver
Shnooky's Cookies, Denver
Simmers & Seasonings (Simmers & Seasonings),
  Lakewood
Southern Tea Co., Denver
Stokes-Ellis Foods Company (Stokes, Ellis), Denver
Suncoa Foods, Inc., Greeley
Tour Ice of Durango, Ind., Durango
T. L. C. Foods, Inc., Denver
Ultimate Performance Products (Sportea), Denver
Vic's Corn Popper, Boulder
Wahatoya Herb (Breathe-Free, Flow-Thru, Geronimo,
  Soothe-Me, Just For Fun), Gardner
Wheat Land Farms (Sam's Snacks), Yuma
White Wave, Inc. (White Wave, Soyfoods Unlimited,
  Tofruzen), Boulder

Miscellaneous

Colorado Peddler, Denver
Dowling Enterprises, Inc. (Dowling's), Denver
Gelato Bravo!, Littleton
Gingerbear House, Inc., The (The Gingerbear House),
  Lakewood
Wheat Unlimited (Wheat Unlimited), Flagler

INDEX

Appetizers & Snacks

Breads

Beverages

Soups, Stews & Chili

Salads

Sauces

Barbecue Sauce 82
Buttermilk/Bleu Cheese Dressing 84
Caribbean Creole Curry Sauce 80
Colorado Salsa 83
Creamy Honey Vanilla Dressing for Fruit 85
Mocha Sundae Sauce 84
Mustard Grill Sauce for Meat or Chicken 80
Peach Spread 85
Roasted Pecan Salad Dressing 83
Savory Yoghurt Dressing 85
Sauce for Roast Pork 81
Spaghetti Sauce 81

Vegetables

Anasazi Beans® and Ham Hocks 94
Apple Raisin Rice Pilaf 101
Apple Stuffing 99
Artichokes Alla Romagna 101
Brazilian Black Beans 97
Chef Mickey's Famous Red Beans 93
Country Style Pinto Beans 89
Crisp Golden Mushrooms 96
Cusat 92
Eggplant Parmesan 96
Fried Beans Deluxe 94
Mexicali Jumping Mushrooms 95
Mexicali Potato Pie 91
Microwaved Baked Apples 98
Refried Anasazi Beans® 95
Scalloped Corn 100
Stuffed Potatoes with Cheese and Chilies 88

Pasta

Chicken Supreme 105
Chili Mac and Cheese Casserole for Kids 108
Fettuccine with Mussels, Mushrooms and Romano Cheese 107
Frankly Noodle Casserole 113
Fresh Tomato Sauce with Pesto 110
La Dolce Ziti 111
Meat Ravioli with Garlic and Olive Oil 109
Pork Meatballs Stroganoff 106
Ravioli Parmigana 112
Salmon Tetrazzini 104
Sliced Eggs 'N Noodles 108
Spinach Ravioli Alfredo 112

Main Dishes

4-Way Grilled Cheese 127
Apple-Shrimp Sauté 145
Bagels Benedict 143
Beef Tenderloin with Vegetable Medley 120
Black Bean Chili Pie 140
Black Bean Tortilla Bake 142
Buffalo with Broccoli Stir-Fry 118
Calico Casserole 148
Cashew Pork Stir-Fry 124
Chicken Santa Fe 128
Chorizo Burrito 149
Crawfish Etoufee 123
Easy Paella 147
Four Corners Rabbitchiladas 119
Garden Burgers 138
Grilled Reuben on Rye 141
Hot Hoagie Sandwich 135
Liver Sauté with Cauliflower Au Gratin 144
Mapo Tofu 139
Maverick Crustless Pizza 137
Mrs. Coors' Sauerbraten 132
Pork Chop and Potato Casserole 127
Pulkogi 121
Ribs 'N Rice 125
Saguache Stir-Fry 116
Sauer-Hot Dogs 130
Shrimp and Scallop Sauté 133
Spanish Beef and Squash Supreme 117
Stir-Fry Chinese Rabbit 126
Stuffed Pork Chops with Mushroom Gravy 131
Suzanne's Stroganoff 145
Taco Dogs 134
Tofu Enchiladas 141
Western-Style Hamburgers 136

Meats & Fish

Baked Trout 156
Barbecued Brisket 181
Batter Fried Fish with Orange Delight Sauce 158
Beer-Broiled Shrimp 160
Beer-Grilled Chops 175
Best Brisket 180
Boeuf Bourguignonne 185
Breaded Lamb Chops 164
Buffalo Chuck Roast 167
Chicken and Grapes 174
Cola Brisket 173
Colorado Lamb Chops and Peppers 167

Desserts